Comfort Pie

Comfort Pie

Kathryn Hawkins

First published in 2012 by
New Holland Publishers Pty Ltd
London • Sydney • Cape Town • Auckland •
www.newhollandpublishers.com
www.newholland.com.au

1/66 Gibbes Street Chatswood NSW 2067 Australia
Garfield House 86–88 Edgware Road London W2 2EA United Kingdom
Wembly Square, First Floor Solan Street Gardens Cape Town 8000 South Africa
218 Lake Road Northcote Auckland New Zealand

A record of this book is held at the British Library.
ISBN: 9781847739988

Publisher: Clare Sayer
Publishing manager: Lliane Clarke
Designer: Geoff Borin
Cover design: Geoff Borin
Production manager: Olga Dementiev
Printer: Toppan Leefung (China) Ltd

10 9 8 7 6 5 4 3 2 1

Follow New Holland Publishers on Facebook:
www.facebook.com/NewHollandPublishers

Contents

Introduction 7

A brief history of pies 9

The basics of pastry making 10

Types of pastry 22

Meat 42

Poultry 82

Fish 102

Vegetables 122

Sweet 148

Bibliography 172

Index 175

The idea for this book came from a conversation I had with my
Mum, so I'd like to dedicate the finished work to her
and thank her for her inspiration.

Introduction

Pie is something I can remember eating and enjoying throughout my childhood. Minced meat, sausage or cheese and potato pies made inexpensive, tasty and filling suppers for our Mother to make us, and at the weekend, for a special treat we would have a homemade apple pie with custard or sometimes vanilla ice cream – we didn't have a freezer, so we would wait in pie-eyed anticipation while Dad went off to the corner shop to buy an icy cardboard packed square of Cornish ice cream before we could tuck in. On every picnic, there was always a pie in some form or other – individual pork, sausage rolls or a wedge of egg and bacon pie were the most memorable.

When we went on holidays to stay with my grandparents in Devon, Grannie Watts would always produce a homegrown-fruit pie at some point – usually rhubarb or blackcurrant – served with luscious clotted cream. And always with homemade, short, buttery pastry – there were no short cuts in those days! – and a quirky blackbird pie funnel sticking out the top. Grannie's sister-in-law Dorothy used to bake for the family café, and a visit to see her on the way to the beach meant that our picnic basket would be embellished with freshly baked, and still warm, savoury pasties. I do remember bad pie experiences just as well though: school dinner pies are certainly amongst the worst ones I have eaten. I can't remember any savoury, just the pudding ones. The pastry was dry, hard and tasteless – mercifully only pastry on the bottom – and the filling or topping was either too sweet, paste-like and flavourless, or so sparse it looked like it had only been shown the pastry!

What is a pie? Well, I think a pie is different things to different people, so for the purposes of this book, I have kept to my own specific boundaries. First and most importantly, it must have pastry as the key ingredient – you'll find no mashed potato tops or other pastry-less pies in this book. Secondly, the pastry should be baked to form a crisp crust or shell – so no steamed pastry. And, finally my pies have either a pastry top and bottom (or all round pastry casing), or are top crust only – this is typically British; if there is bottom crust (like an American pie) it must support a good hearty portion of filling and be topped in some way. Apart from that they can be any shape, size, in or out of a tin or dish, and made up with any type of pastry.

Pastry is a vital constituent of a really good pie, but the filling is of equal importance. While I have been writing my recipes, quite by chance, I was asked to be a judge on a panel for the Perthshire region of the Scottish Association of Meat Traders Steak Pie and Speciality Pie competition. I met some experienced pie making butchers who explained the techniques they used to get the right amount of filling in a dish but still achieve a good crisp puff pastry layer on top. We had a fine old time looking at the differing pastry textures and tasting the meat and gravy, and it was a very interesting, and extremely timely experience for me. On balance, it was the pastry that let most pies down, and then seasoning came in a close second.

I have tried to come up with pies for every occasion in the recipe section. To start with you'll find recipes for different types of pastry if you fancy making your own - if you have sufficient time, I do recommend you try and have a go. There is something very satisfying about making your own pastry and the taste and texture of the baked result is far superior to anything readymade. However, time is of the essence, so I do state the quantity of pastry each recipe makes to enable you to substitute in a readymade version if you need to.

There are 70 glorious pie recipes to follow the basic pastries which are divided up into different chapters depending on the filling, and you'll find recipes for large family pies as well as individual ones, using a variety of different types of pastry.

Before you start cooking though, you should read my tips and techniques on general pie and pastry making. Making a large meat filled pie is quite an investment on time and ingredients, so it seems a shame not to get a good result because of a simple problem in putting the pie together.

I hope you enjoy the book. I certainly had fun making all the pies and sharing them with friends and family, watching faces light up as I produced my latest pastry creation – pies are a very sociable food and everyone seems to appreciate a good one.

Happy pie making!

Kathryn

A brief history of pies

Pies are recognised and baked all over the world in many shapes, forms and sizes, but many languages offer no exact translation of the word; this leads food historians to believe that pies evolved in Europe, especially in northern regions. When I first came to write on the subject, every book I own on the subject of British food history is littered with references to pies dating back to Medieval times, but in other books of global culinary history they occur only as introduced dishes. In *Larousse Gastronomique* under the entry for "pie", it reads: "The French have adopted the word for the classic British and American pies". I like to deduce from my research, therefore, that the pie, is a very British dish, which we have shared with our cousins across the Atlantic Ocean! Pies are also popular in Australia and New Zealand.

Pies of old were primarily a means to cook, keep and transport an assortment of fillings – the tough, dough casing was never eaten. It is thought that the word pie (pâté in Medieval English) has an ornithological derivation and comes from magpie – a bird with the habit of collecting things. There are many historical references to pies of old throughout culinary history. As with many familiar things, pies can also be dated back to the Egyptians.

Humble pie dates back to Medieval times. Now a common saying, it evolved in households where the folk at the top of the pecking order would get the prime cuts, and the poor workers would get a pie full of entrails and offal – you'll find my version of this recipe inside this book. Cornish tin miners used to carry a pastry with savoury mixture at one end and fruit or jam (jelly) at the other in a roughly honed dough which was discarded once the insides were eaten – this was the original Cornish pasty. It was during the times of the Tudors, that pastry, or *paste* as it was known then, really became part of the dish called "pie". Eggs were added as well as cold fats like butter and suet, and a more refined wheat flour was used for baking. Standing pies, like our raised pies of today, sound truly magnificent – like pieces of art you could actually eat. Pastry animals, birds, leaves and foliage were embossed or stuck all over the outside – just like we do today with our (crude in comparison) pastry cutters, and the patterns on the outside often depicted the filling within. For banquets and feasts heraldic emblems, coats of arms and other family emblems were also used as edible decor.

Shortcrust pastry recipes were recorded as early as 1545, but it wasn't for another 50 years or so that flakier recipes started to appear written down. I've often wondered how puff pastry was first discovered – did someone forget to add the fat to the dough and then try to incorporate it afterwards?

It has been recorded that flaky pastry was an Arabic invention of around 1500. At the same time the Turkish were making filo (*phyllo* meaning leaf) sheet pastries for savoury and sweet dishes, and their rule over parts of Eastern Europe meant that this pastry was adapted by the Hungarians and Austrians to make their strudels.

By the end of the sixteenth century, pastry was widely made and eaten all over the world. The first American pie recipes began to appear in the late eighteenth century where fat was rubbed into the flour for a fine texture and some rolled in to give a good flaky crust. American pies are most usually bottom-crust only, which the British often refer to as a tart. Rarely have pies gone out of fashion and with our renewed enthusiasm for baking, comfort food and getting back in the kitchen, we're all cooking like never before and pies are everywhere!

The basics of pastry making

There is no real mystery to turning out a good pie, but there are a few basics that you need to understand before you get started. Even if you're using readymade pastry, you'll still get a better result if you follow the same guidelines. I don't think you can rush a pie and expect it to look or taste good. A pie is a real labour of love, and whoever you're serving it up to will love you all the more for taking the time to get it tasting and looking right. I think a pie is an impressive beast whatever the occasion, and it seems a shame to rush it and then have it not turn out to your best advantage. With this in mind, I've put together some tips and techniques as well as my basic "pie rules" and general information to help you achieve your perfect, homely and satisfying, deliciously perfect pie. Read on pie enthusiasts.

Pastry ingredients

1) Flour

Provides the main bulk and structure of any pastry. Wheat flour contains proteins which form gluten, and gluten helps the pastry firm up and crisp when baked. Plain or all purpose white wheat flour is the most commonly used for a standard shortcrust pastry, with the wholewheat (brown) version offering a healthier, more wholesome crust. Wheat flour with added raising agent (self raising flour) is used for a softer textured pastry like suet crust, but if you fancy experimenting, it can be used for shortcrust and will make a crumbly textured pastry which merges into the filling during baking and offers a less pronounced crust.

If you are wheat intolerant, you can use gluten free flours – I have included suggestions and recipes. Pastry made with a gluten free flour will have a different texture but can still provide a perfectly adequate casing for many different fillings. Remember to choose a flour that will combine well with filling flavours for example, some flours like gram (chickpea) have a beany, earthy flavour and are best suited to savoury fillings.

For pastries with layers and flakes (flaky, rough puff or puff) or when a more robust or free standing pastry case is required (hot water crust), a wheat flour with a higher protein content and thus more gluten, is often used. Choose strong plain (bread) or white bread flour for a firmer, crisper result. However, a bread flour with too high a protein content can make a tough pastry that shrinks. Standard plain (all purpose) flour can be used for these pastries too and the results will be slightly softer and flakier in texture; the type you choose is down personal experimentation and taste.

As with all pastry ingredients, make sure you use fresh flour for best results. Store flours in their bags, well sealed, in a cool dry place.

2) Fat

Fat determines the texture and flavour of a pastry. Butter, vegetable shortening and lard are the most commonly used, but vegetable oils can also be used. Weigh or measure fat carefully as too much can make the pastry greasy and short (difficult to handle), while not enough will make a hard, dry pastry. Usually lard and butter are used together for best results, the former gives a short, crisp texture while the latter adds flavour. You will see recipes using combinations or a single fat. Choosing a hard vegetable fat is down to personal taste and health preferences. Choose a fat with no (unsalted) or a low salt content so that you can control the seasoning of the pastry – see notes on salt below. Avoid low fat spreads or any fat with an added water content ("spreadable") as they will alter the texture of the finished pastry.

Shredded beef or vegetable suet is used for suet crust pastries. It's down to personal taste which you prefer to use; personally, I prefer beef suet with savoury and vegetable suet with sweet fillings or delicate flavours like vegetables, fish and poultry.

If you want to experiment with different oils, make sure you choose an oil that is suitable for cooking. Delicate flavoured oils such as extra virgin olive or nut oils are not heat resistant – they are used to flavour a finished dish rather than cook with. However, when blended with a more robust oil like sunflower, they can be used for flavouring purposes. Remember that the colour and flavour of an oil will affect the final taste of the pie, so it is worth choosing a blander flavoured vegetable oil if you don't want the pastry to dominate the pie filling.

Try to get the fat at the right temperature before blending with your flour. Rock hard fat, straight from the fridge, is too difficult to blend, but if it is too soft, the fat has already started to melt and won't combine with the flour correctly. Don't be tempted to blast fat in the microwave in order to soften it in a hurry; more than likely, it will get too soft and will ruin the pastry. Ideally, take the fat out of the fridge about 30 mins before using to make sure the fat is firm and cool, not soft and oily.

3) Liquids

Water is the most commonly used liquid in pastry making and acts as a binding agent bringing the flour and fat together to make a dough. In general, 1 tsp cold water is used per 25g (1oz) flour for a short pastry, and 1 Tbsp water per 25g (1oz) flour for suet or flaky pastries. Sometimes milk, cream or yogurt is used instead of water to give a richer, shorter, more flavoursome pastry crust. Fruit juice can be used in sweet pastries to give more flavour – usually citrus juices are used with finely grated rind for increased zestiness.

Liquid is always added cold to a pastry with the exception of hot water crust, where it is heated with the fat until melted and very hot. Where egg is added (see following notes) the liquid content is reduced.

4) Egg

Usually only the yolk is added to pastry dough to enrich it in flavour, texture and colour. The extra liquid provided by adding the yolk to the mixture means that you will need to reduce the quantity of liquid you add in order to avoid an over-wet dough. Well-beaten whole egg is widely used in pastry making and brushed on raw pastry as a glaze. Beaten egg white and a sprinkling of sugar gives a crisp coating to a sweet pie, whereas egg yolk on its own gives an ultra-rich finish.

5) Salt

Adding this everyday condiment will help bring out the flavour of your savoury and your sweet pastries. Measure salt correctly, especially when adding to a pastry being used for a sweet filling –follow the guidelines stated in the recipe. Season the filling carefully too, keeping in mind that your pastry already has a salt content.

6) Sugar

Sugar is added in small amounts to sweet pastries. White, fine, caster (superfine) or icing (confectioner's) sugars are most commonly used as these are most easily blended in a pastry dough, but soft light brown and dark sugars can be used for a more rustic pastry, and will also give a more caramelised flavour and colour to a baked pie crust – definitely worth experimenting with. Sweet pies are also often sprinkled with sugar to give a crust either before baking or just before serving. Demerara sugar gives an added crunchy finish to a pastry crust before baking.

7) Other ingredients

To give a standard recipe a "twist" you can add small amounts of seasonings and flavourings to your mixture. Chopped fresh herbs, dried herbs or spices can be used successfully in a savoury pastry, and cinnamon, ginger, nutmeg and ground mixed spice are great with fruit fillings, as are finely grated citrus zests. Cocoa powder can be substituted in to a recipe instead of some of the flour content to give a chocolate flavoured pastry – add some sugar as well to reduce the bitterness. Liquid extracts or essences like vanilla, almond or coffee can be used for flavour – add these before adding any other liquid to avoid making the pastry too wet. Ground nuts and small whole seeds can be used in addition to or instead of some of the flour for flavour and texture, or for reasons of intolerance to wheat.

The rules for pastry making

- The most important factor in pastry making is temperature. For all the pastries covered in this book, except hot water crust, you need to keep everything cool. Don't handle pastry more than you have to and use only your finger tips to rub the fat into the flour – if you suffer with poor circulation like me you'll have cold hands which is regarded as a positive when it comes to pastry making! Rich short pastries and flaky pastries will benefit from resting in a cool place or the fridge before rolling and shaping again to firm up the fat content.

- If you prefer a short cut to rubbing in by hand, you can use a hand held mixer or food processor. It is always best to work the fat into the flour in short bursts, and the same with adding liquid, otherwise there is a possibility that the pastry can become too over-mixed or processed and will be tough as a result. Refer to the manufacturer's instruction booklet for the correct settings and attachments.

- Add liquid in gradual, small amounts to avoid making the pastry dough too wet – if the mixture is too sticky it will not only be difficult to handle, it will dry out and harden too much on cooking. Avoid adding extra flour when rolling out if your pastry is too sticky as this will alter the proportion of ingredients and have a detrimental effect on the texture of the pastry by toughening the texture.

- Roll pastry in one direction. The easiest way is to roll it away from you - then turn and roll it in the same "away from you" direction. For rounds of pastry, form the pastry into a ball first, then rotate as you roll, pinching together any cracks that appear on the edge. Being methodical with your turning and rolling technique means you are building a good, even structure to your pastry, particularly important for flaky pastry making when the rolling process helps form the flaky layers for the finished pastry. Use as little flour as possible to avoid drying out your pastry, and keep rolling to a minimum to avoid over-handling.

  Admittedly, some pastries are more difficult to handle. For example those with a high fat content or low or no gluten. In this instance, you are better to try and loosen the pastry with a long, broad palette knife after every rolling, and either slide the pastry round on the work top, or if this is too difficult, roll in a methodical fashion up and down and then side to side, to achieve an even thickness.

- Most recipes in this book require you to roll out the pastry thinly. This means to a thickness of around 3-5mm (¼inch).

- Take care not to stretch the pastry to fit the tin or mould as this will mean that the pastry will shrink back during cooking and may become misshapen.

- Most recipes call for freshly made or shaped pastry to be rested or chilled before filling or baking. Always cover the pastry in clear wrap or if in a block, wrap in greaseproof paper. This will prevent a skin or crust forming, and will stop the pastry drying out or picking up other flavours.

- Pastry is best cooked in a hot oven so that the fat doesn't "melt out" of the mixture but instead coats the flour particles quickly enabling the dough to cook to a crisp. Everyone's oven heats up differently so if you are concerned that your oven may not be heating up correctly, it is worth putting an oven thermometer on the centre shelf of the oven in order to double check the temperature. This is the best way to ensure you are cooking at the correct temperature.

- Short and flaky pastries can be stored for 2-5 days in the fridge if you don't want to use them immediately. You should wrap them well to avoid picking up flavours from other ingredients and to prevent a skin or crust forming on the outside. Similarly, these pastries freeze well. Wrap tightly and freeze for up to 6 months, then allow to defrost, still in the wrappings, in the fridge for a few hours until ready to use. Hot water crust pastry must be used while warm and fresh otherwise it will be too hard to handle. Allow a pastry to "warm up" slightly if it has been stored in the fridge – let it stand at room temperature for about 20 mins before using.

A word on readymade pastries

Some pastries are simply too time consuming to make and sometimes there just aren't enough hours in the day to make your own pastry, so for those occasions we turn to readymade pastries. Shortcrust wheat flour pastry is available in fresh and frozen forms, for sweet and savoury baking, in different flavours, and in block or ready rolled sheets. While this is my least favourite of the "readymades" (I'm not too keen on the flavour) it is a perfectly adequate compromise to making fresh. You do have to follow the guidelines on the packet though regarding using and resting times otherwise the pastry shrinks.

Readymade puff pastry is extremely popular and desirable with cooks and chefs alike; it really is a valuable substitute to the real thing. Available fresh, frozen, in blocks or ready rolled, mixed fat and all-butter, I have had no failures or disappointments using these products. Again read the guidelines given by the manufacturer for best results.

There are two other pastry types I use in this book which I have not attempted to make, and they are filo and brick. Both are extremely thin, wafer like, leaf pastries which cook to a fine crisp. They are typically used in Mediterranean, North African and Middle Eastern cookery. Filo pastry is now widely available in delicatessens, grocers' shops or supermarkets in fresh or frozen forms. It is usually wrapped in clear film and packaged in a long box. Size of sheet varies, and I find the bigger sheets (around 38 x 37cm /15¾ x 12inch) easier to work with; if only smaller sheets are available, double up or overlap to give a bigger working area. Filo pastry dries out quickly, so keep unused sheets wrapped up or covered in damp kitchen paper. It is lower in fat than other pastries and is usually brushed with melted butter or oil before using in a pie in order to give a crisp finish; without the fat filo is rather dry and leathery once cooked – beaten egg can be used to crisp up pastry however for a lower fat alternative. Filo pastry pies are best eaten hot or warm when the pastry is still crisp.

Brick pastry is a more specialist pastry but worth tracking down. It is used in North African pastries. Also called *feuilles de brick, brik, briouat* and *oarka,* depending on where and how it is used. It comes in the form of wafer thin rounds or squares of pastry which can be baked or fried. Unlike filo it is not "greased" before using but still cooks to a delightful crisp. I have included a couple of recipes in my book which use this pastry to show you the techniques involved, but also give instructions for using filo pastry as an alternative.

Pie making tips and techniques

Once you've made your pastry or bought some, next you need to know how to make up your pie. There are several different ways you can present a pie depending on how much pastry you want to use. Being a huge pastry fan, I like my pies to have a bottom and a top, and I always feel a bit cheated if there's nothing at the bottom of the dish to hold my filling in place; but that's just personal preference and perhaps a touch of greediness too!

Individual recipes in the book give basic instructions for the pie stated, but below are some general pointers to help you achieve a good result.

1) PIE MAKING EQUIPMENT
The good news is that you don't really need anything special to make a pie.

i) Dishes, tins and moulds: metallic or enamel pie dishes or tins come in various sizes and are reasonably priced; they are ideal for double crust pies as they conduct the heat well and help firm up the pastry base. Ceramic dishes are good for top crust pies; they should have a wide rim to that you can attach the pastry to the dish with ease. Pie plates have a wide rim and a gently dipping middle; they can be made of ceramic, enamel or metal. Double crust pies are easier to cut made in a pie plate, but you don't get much filling per portion. If lots of filling, choose a deep earthenware pie dish; oval, square or round in shape, available in many sizes, these are the dishes for a pastry topped pie. For more specialist and fancy pies, you'll find metal pie moulds and long loaf tins with hinged sides for easy release. Some moulds have embossed and decorative sides that leave an impression on the pastry when it is cooked. Pies look pretty impressive baked in these tins, but these tins are more expensive to buy. Loose bottomed and spring clip tins are less expensive and less fancy but do enable you to produce a perfect free standing pie with the minimum of fuss.

ii) **Pie funnel (pie bird):** most usually made of ceramic or porcelain, and shaped like a pointed chimney or a bird with its beak open. More contemporary funnels are available in bright colours made of silicone, and there are also novelty ones out there if you fancy starting a collection! Pie funnels let out steam from the pie filling as it bakes and help prevent the pastry top becoming soggy by giving it a little support, keeping it slightly away from the filling. You can use a greased large metal piping nozzle if you don't have a specialist funnel, or make your own by rolling up a double thickness of aluminium foil into a short, narrow tube.

iii) **Rolling pin and metal ruler:** use a heavy, long rolling pin for best results. Wood is the most traditional, but marble is also good as it helps keep the pastry cool as well. Avoid any rolling pin with grooves or pits that will mark your pastry as you roll, and keep it clean to avoid transferring flavours. I have a 30cm (12inch) metal ruler that I find useful for kitchen use. It gives a good cutting edge and also acts as a palette knife helping release pastry from the work surface for easy turning.

iv) **Flour shaker or dredger:** useful but not essential. Does ensure you only get only a fine sifting of flour on your work surface when you are ready to roll out your pastry. Make sure the flour inside the shaker gets changed regularly – ideally, put only a small amount of flour in your shaker each time you use it. A sieve works just as well.

v) **Baking beans:** small reusable marble-like ceramic "beans" which are used for weighing down an unfilled pastry case during baking. During baking, the pastry sets in position with the beans on top, and once the pastry sets they then can be removed and the empty pastry case can be put back in the oven to finish baking. You can use just as easily raw pulses or rice to achieve the same result.

vi) **Pastry board or mat:** marble slabs are expensive and heavy, but are perfect for keeping your pastry cool as you work. I have a cold, north facing kitchen so this is not something I ever need to consider, but I have certainly used marble in the past when conditions have been warmer. Pastry mats are reasonably priced and help you remove pastry after rolling, reducing the risk of tearing it.

vii) **Work surface:** do remember to make sure your work surface is thoroughly clean before you roll out your pastry – a spray of food-safe antibacterial spray and a good wipe away before you get started is all you need to do. If you have chips or marks in your work surface, keep in mind that these will get transferred on to your pastry if you roll out on such a surface.

Pie funnels or pie birds are usually made of ceramic or porcelain, and shaped like a pointed chimney or a bird with its beak open.

2) TOP CRUST PIE

This type of pie is most usually made in a deep pie dish. Put the filling in the dish so that it is quite full and a little rounded on top – if you don't have quite enough filling, use a pie funnel to stop the pastry sagging.

Roll out the pastry of choice to the required thickness, 5cm (2inch) wider than the pie dish. Wet the rim of the pie dish with water. Cut 2.5cm (1inch) wide strips of pastry from the outer edge of the rolled pastry and press them neatly on to the rim of the dish to cover the rim completely. Brush the pastry rim with water or beaten egg. Lift the remaining pastry on to the rolling pin and lay it over the pie dish. If you are using a pie funnel, you need to cut a cross in the centre of the pastry first. Trim off the excess pastry with a sharp knife held at a slight angle away from the dish. Seal the pastry firmly by either pressing with your thumb and forefinger or using the prongs of a fork.

It is important to get a good seal on your pastry and "knocking up" the edges is an extra insurance policy towards achieving this. Using a kitchen knife blade, make horizontal shallow cuts in the side of the pastry edges to give the appearance of layers or pages in a book and merge the two layers together to seal. Do this all round the rim of pastry.

Pastry trimmings can be gathered, rolled and used as decoration on top of the pie lid. Cut a slit in the centre of the pie crust for the steam to escape, and glaze as directed. I prefer to bake all my pies in their dish on a baking tray, just in case any filling bubbles out during cooking. Some cooks like to preheat the baking tray in the oven as it warms up so that the pie goes straight on to a hot tray and gets cooking quicker; this is supposed to help cook a pastry bottom more crisply, but I'm not entirely sure it really makes that much difference.

3) DOUBLE CRUSTERS

My favourite pie, one with a pastry top and bottom. Most usually made with shortcrust, but you can use one of the flaky pastries, and sometimes you'll see a shortcrust pastry bottom with a flaky pastry lid. Divide the pastry in two, making one piece slightly bigger than the other. Roll the larger piece to the required thickness, to 2.5cm (1inch) bigger than the combined measurement of the diameter and sides of the dish – if you're using a shallow pie plate, then simply use the inverted pie plate as your guide. Lift the remaining pastry on to the rolling pin and lay it over the pie dish. If your chosen dish has sides, carefully fit the pastry into it, easing the pastry in place on the sides, taking care not to stretch or tear the pastry – if the pastry is short, you can patch the pastry together again by pinching and moulding the pastry, sealing over any joins, and pressing them evenly to make a smooth case. Make sure there are no air pockets between the sides and the pastry. Trim the pastry as necessary.

Add your chosen cold filling, slightly rounding the surface, or use a pie funnel if necessary. Brush the pastry rim with water or beaten egg. Roll out the remaining pastry to form the lid, making sure it is about 1cm (½inch) bigger than the pie dish, and lift the lid into position using your rolling pin. Cover the pie and seal the edge. Trim as necessary and seal as described above. Decorate with trimmings if liked. Cut a slit in the centre of the pie crust for the steam to escape, and glaze as directed.

4) BOTTOM CRUST PIE

Most usually made with a shortcrust pastry which is usually baked without a filling (baking blind). However, I do include a few pies where the filling is baked in the pastry case and then given a topping which requires further baking. Loose-bottomed or spring clip (springform) tins are useful for making pastry cases that you want to be free-standing; for best results, lightly grease the tin and then base-line it with baking parchment. You can also use ceramic, shallow-sided pie or flan dishes for this type of pie, and serve your pie straight from the dish. Again, if you line the bottom of the dish with baking parchment, you will be able to cut the pie and get it out of the dish more easily.

Roll out the pastry to the required thickness to the combined measurements of the diameter plus the sides of the tin or dish. Using a rolling pin, lift the pastry and lower it into the tin or dish. Carefully fit the pastry to the sides, easing it into place, taking care not to stretch or tear the pastry – if the pastry is short, you can patch the pastry together again by pinching and moulding the pastry, sealing over any joins, pressing them evenly to make a smooth case. Make sure there are no air pockets between the sides and the pastry. Trim the pastry as necessary, leaving approx.½cm (5mm) over the rim of the tin or dish.

To bake a pastry case "blind", cut a piece of baking parchment the same shape as your pastry case, but slightly larger all round. Place it in the centre of the pastry case and half-fill with ceramic baking beans or raw rice. Bake as directed in your recipe until set. Carefully remove the parchment and beans, prick the base with a fork and return to the oven as directed to enable the base to dry out.

5) INDIVIDUAL PIES

For making smaller pies, the principles are the same as above, just scaled down. Do take care not to stretch the pastry to fit the tins. Large pastry cutters or saucers make the perfect stencils for lining and covering round tins. For very small tins, simply break off a small knob of pastry, roll it into a ball and press it into each tin, then use your fingers to push and ease the pastry up the sides.

6) RAISED PIE

Various pie recipes, of different shapes and sizes, using hot water crust pastry are given in the book along with full instructions for assembling them. The most important thing to remember when using this type of pastry is that it sets as it cools and becomes harder to work with. Keep the part of the pastry that is not being worked with covered under a cloth or an upturned bowl to reduce the cooling time.

Preparing the pastry
for 'baking blind'.

7) Pie fillings

Because pastry has a high fat content it melts easily and becomes greasy, and therefore, most usually pie fillings are cold when the pie is assembled. Pastry requires cooking at a relatively high temperature for a reasonably short time so if your filling is raw you need to ensure that it will cook thoroughly in the time it takes to cook the pastry. For this reason, many fillings are cooked and cooled in advance. Slow cooked meats such as stewing beef and mutton are casseroled first and then cooled before being used as a filling. Once they are cold, scrape off any fat that forms on the top to make the filling less greasy. These fillings benefit from a "second cooking" when reheated under a pie crust as they have more flavour and become meltingly tender.

Try to avoid adding too much gravy, sauce or cooking liquor to a pie filing, especially if the pie has a pastry bottom; excess liquid will be absorbed by raw pastry and prevent it from becoming crisp, and it may also leak out over the sides of the dish, spoiling the appearance of the finished pie and result in insufficient filling retained under the pastry crust.

As with any food that requires reheating, make sure your filling cools as quickly as possible and is then covered and stored in the fridge until required for pie making. Always reheat pie fillings thoroughly – a digital food probe or thermometer inserted into the centre of a cooked pie is an ideal way to dispel any doubts you may have about internal temperature.

If using a chilled filling, let the filling stand at room temperature for about 20 mins before cooking to that it reheats quicker. Delicate textured pie fillings like fish, eggs and soft fruit are only lightly cooked beforehand or used raw in order to preserve flavour and texture.

8) Pie decorations and finishing techniques

You can transform the top of any pie from something very plain to something completely over the top by using up your pastry trimmings and making various shapes and decorations. There is a huge range of pastry cutters available these days, in many sizes. Leaves used to be the most traditional of shapes, but now you can find cutters to reflect just about any filling: I've got fishes, birds, pigs, sheep and cows for my pies, as well as a selection of fruit and vegetables, and even some bugs and beasties (perfect for children's parties!). Pastry stars are festive and seasonal, and hearts make any pie extra special; you can spell out the filling or personalise a pie with alphabet cutters, or make up your own designs by cutting round a cardboard stencil or template. Simply stick pastry shapes on to the pie top using water or beaten egg and then glaze along with the rest of the pastry top. For a splash of colour, leave the pastry decorations unglazed before baking and then once baked, paint them with a light brushing of food colouring – looks great on a cherry pie: simply paint small pastry rounds red, and leaf shapes green.

Types of Pastry

Shortcrust Pastry

Ingredients

250g (9oz) plain
    (all purpose) flour
Pinch of salt
125g (4 ½ oz) half white fat
    (lard or vegetable equivalent)
    and half block margarine or
    unsalted butter, cut into small
    pieces
About 4 Tbsp cold water

A widely used "short" pastry that is easily made, quick and simple to use and forms the base, top and sides of many savoury and sweet dishes.

1. Mix the flour and salt together and add the pieces of fat.

2. Using both hands, rub the fat into the flour between finger and thumb tips. In a short while, you will see the mixture is well blended and resembles fresh breadcrumbs.

3. Sprinkle the water evenly over the pastry crumbs and stir with a round bladed knife until the mixture comes together in large lumps. Using one hand, scoop up the pieces and knead lightly for a few seconds to make a firm, smooth dough.

4. You can use this pastry straight away but it is better to leave it to stand or "rest" for 15 mins in the bowl so that the flour can absorb the fat. For later use, wrap and chill for up to 2 days, or freeze.

Variations

- Wholewheat and spelt – follow the basic recipe but you may need to add a little more water to bring the mixture together. Blend half white flour with wholewheat flour to give a lighter crust.

- If you want to make a slighter richer pastry, increase the proportion of fat to 150g (5oz) to 250g (9oz) flour – you will need less water, approx. 3 Tbsp.

- For a simple sweet variation, add 3 Tbsp caster (superfine) sugar to the rubbed in mixture.

- Fat reduced – it is possible to make shortcrust using less fat and more water – use 75g (2½oz) to the amount of flour above and you will need approx. 6 Tbsp water. The result will be a firmer, more chewy pastry which is perfect for containing gravy- or sauce-rich fillings.

- Nut pastry – replace 50g (2oz) of the flour with ground or finely chopped unsalted nuts such as walnuts, hazelnuts, almonds or pecans. Can be used with savoury and sweet dishes, and has a softer texture than an all wheat shortcrust.

Wheat Free and Gluten Free Shortcrust

Makes: 450g (1lb) Preparation: 10 mins

Ingredients

125g (4 ½ oz) brown rice flour

125g (4 ½ oz) soya flour

½ tsp gluten free baking powder

125g (4 ½ oz) unsalted butter
    or margarine

4 Tbsp cold water

There are so many varieties of gluten free flour available. Without gluten, pastry is much softer and more crumbly in texture than traditional shortcrust; it needs to be handled a bit differently. If only wheat gluten is a problem, you can make a very tasty pastry using finely ground oats.

1. Mix the flours and baking powder together. Cut the fat into small pieces and toss into the flour.

2. Using both hands, rub the fat into the flour between finger and thumb tips. In a short while, you will see the mixture is well blended and resembles fresh breadcrumbs.

3. Sprinkle the water evenly over the pastry crumbs and stir with a round bladed knife until the mixture begins to come together in large lumps. Using one hand, scoop up the pieces and knead lightly for a few seconds to make a soft dough.

4. This pastry is ready to use straight away but it is much softer than other pastries and you may find it only suitable for lining a tin at this stage. For later use, wrap and chill for up to 2 days, or freeze. Chilling will firm up the pastry dough and give you more options for using it as per your chosen recipe.

Variations

- For an oat pastry replace the 2 flours above with 250g (9oz) porridge oats which you blitz in a blender or food processor to make a fine powder.

- For a sweet version, add 2-3tsp caster (superfine) or light brown sugar to the blended pastry crumbs.

- Replace soya flour with gram (chickpea) flour for a really nutty, savoury pastry; buckwheat flour will also give a nutty, earthy flavour. Both flours are best suited to savoury dishes. You will need to add more water with different gluten free flours as the absorption rate varies between different types.

- You can also use finely ground nuts as one of the flours in the recipe – ground almond or chestnuts make a deliciously rich, crumbly pastry for a sweet dish.

Suet Crust

Ingredients

200g (7oz) self raising flour

¾ tsp salt

100g (3 ½ oz) shredded beef or
   vegetable suet

150ml (¼ pt) cold water

This is a pastry from "yesteryear". It went quite out of fashion for several years due to increased health awareness, but now there is a vegetable alternative to traditional beef suet. This means that suet crust, the easiest-of-all pastries to make, is back on the menu. Vegetable suet is also lower in fat but can be used in the same way.

1. Mix together the flour, salt and suet. Add enough cold water, mixing at the same time, to make a light, elastic dough.

2. Turn on to a lightly floured surface and knead very gently until smooth.

3. This pastry should be used straight away as the raising agent will begin activating once the flour is mixed with water. Suet crust pastry can be used for sweet and savoury dishes and can be steamed as well as baked.

Variations

- Use the same quantity plain (all purpose) flour if you prefer and add 2½tsp baking powder

- Use wholewheat self raising flour or spelt flour plus baking powder for a more wholesome pastry, but you will probably need to add a bit more water.

- Add chopped herbs or spices to the mixture for flavoured doughs. Finely grated citrus rind gives a nice tangy twist for a sweet pastry crust.

Oil Pastry

Makes: 525g (1lb 2½oz)   Preparation: 10 mins plus resting

Ingredients

350g (12oz) plain
   (all purpose) flour
½ tsp salt
115ml (4fl.oz) sunflower or
   vegetable oil
4 Tbsp cold water

A type of shortcrust pastry made using a vegetable oil instead of hard fat. It is more difficult to work with than standard hard fat-based shortcrust but offers different flavour options. Take into account that the oil you choose will affect the colour and flavour of your finished dish. Use nut oils sparingly as they overheat during intensive cooking - they are best blended with a more heat tolerant, neutral tasting oil such as sunflower.

Note: This is a slightly more greasy pastry than one made with solid fat, and it lends itself better to savoury recipes rather than sweet. You may find it difficult to roll as it is inclined to stick to the rolling pin, therefore you may find it easier to patch pieces together when lining a tin. A good solution to patching a top crust together is to cut out shapes of pastry using a cutter, and overlap them on top of the pie filling to form a layer.

1. Mix together the flour and salt together in a bowl. Make a well in the centre and add the oil. Mix until well blended.

2. Gradually blend in the water until the mixture comes together to form a firm dough.

3. Turn on to a lightly floured surface and knead very gently until smooth. Rest for 10 mins before using

Variations

- Heat tolerant cold pressed rapeseed oil and standard olive oil will add more flavour to your pastry.

- If you want to enhance the nutty flavour in a dish, replace 2 tsp of a standard vegetable oil with walnut, hazelnut or sesame seed oil. Nut and seed oils are not heat tolerant so use no more than this quantity otherwise the flavour will be lost or affected.

- Replace white flour with wholewheat or spelt for a more wholesome pastry.

- It is difficult to make a decent gluten free pastry using oil as it becomes very greasy, but some success can be had by blending buckwheat flour with brown rice flour and using sunflower oil.

Soft Cheese Pastry

Makes: 500g (1lb 1½oz) Preparation: 10 mins plus chilling

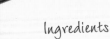

Ingredients

150g (5oz) unsalted butter, softened

150g (5oz) full fat soft cheese

200g (7oz) plain (all purpose) flour

Pinch of salt

There are several ways you can make cheese pastry depending on how cheesy you want the flavour of your pastry to be; recipes are usually based on shortcrust. Below are 2 variations ranging from the mild to the more flavoured.

Note: This is a very short pastry which can be difficult to work, so chilling is essential. It has a delicious melt-in-the-mouth texture, and slight flakiness that will make making it worth the effort. It requires a short cooking time at a high temperature so is only suitable for fillings that require little cooking or heating through.

1. In a mixing bowl, beat together the butter and soft cheese until well blended. Sift the flour and salt on top. Stir until evenly mix, then use your hands to bring the mixture together to form a firmish dough.

2. Turn onto a floured surface and knead gently until smooth – you may need to use more flour with this pastry as it is quite sticky. Wrap and chill for 2 hours before using.

Variations:
- Add chopped herbs for extra flavour in a savoury pie.
- Replace white flour with wholewheat or spelt flour for a more wholesome flavour.

Double Cheese Pastry

Makes: 425g (14½oz)   Preparation: 10 mins plus chilling

Very cheesy, this pastry will add extra savouriness to meat, chicken, fish and vegetarian pies.

1. In a mixing bowl, beat together the butter with the soft cheese and egg yolk. Sift the flour on top and add the grated cheese and salt. Stir until evenly mixed, then use your hands to bring the mixture together to form a firm dough

2. Turn on to a lightly floured surface and knead lightly until smooth, then wrap and chill for 1 hour before using.

Variations:

- Add chopped chives to either recipe for a cheese and onion pastry.
- A pinch of dry mustard added to the flour helps bring out the cheese flavour, and 1 tsp smoked paprika adds a touch of colour and smokiness to a cheesy pastry. Ground cumin or whole cumin seeds give an extra spicy twist to this pastry.

Ingredients

75g (2 ½ oz) unsalted butter, softened
75g (2 ½ oz) full fat soft cheese
1 egg yolk
175g (6oz) plain (all purpose) flour
75g (2 ½ oz) freshly grated Parmesan cheese
½ tsp salt

Pâte Sucrée (Sugar Pastry)

Makes: 450g (1lb) Preparation: 20 mins plus chilling

Ingredients

200g (7oz) plain
(all purpose) flour
¼ tsp salt
3 medium egg yolks
100g (3 ½ oz) unsalted butter
100g (3 ½ oz) caster
(superfine) sugar

A French enriched shortcrust pastry which can be rolled thin and holds its shape well. It has a crisp texture that melts in the mouth with butteriness. Pâte sucrée is the pastry traditionally used for continental pâtisserie. It is best made with white flour.

1. Sift the flour and salt directly on to the work surface in a pyramid shape.

2. Make an indent in the top and add the egg yolks. Cut the butter into small pieces and place on top. Sprinkle over the sugar.

3. Using a palette knife, cover the top with flour from each side of the pile. Using the fingertips of one hand, pinch the dry and wet ingredients together until all the flour is incorporated and the ingredients are well blended, making sure you keep bringing all the ingredients back into a pile as you work them together.

4. Work the dough quickly and lightly to make a smooth dough, and form into a ball. Wrap and chill for at least 1 hour before using.

Variations:

- Some recipes include 2.5–5ml (½–1tsp) good quality vanilla for added flavour; you may prefer to add this extract or try good quality almond extract.
- If you want to add further flavours to your pastry try adding finely grated unwaxed citrus zest or ground spices such as ginger, nutmeg, cinnamon or mixed spice.

Hot Water Crust Pastry

Makes: 800g (1lb 12oz)   Preparation: 10 mins plus resting

This is a classic free standing pie pastry associated with lots of pies, from the everyday picnic pork or fruit pies to the gloriously elaborate raised game pies of celebration banquets. It is mixed with boiling water which makes it pliable to mould, and as it cools it sets in shape and becomes firm. It is best made with white flour.

1. Mix the flour and salt together in a heatproof mixing bowl, and make a well in the centre.

2. Put the fat in a saucepan with the water. Heat gently until melted and then bring to the boil.

3. Remove from the heat and quickly pour into the well all in one go. Working quickly, mix the ingredients together using a wooden spoon until well blended.

4. When just cool enough to touch, use one hand to bring the dough together and knead until smooth and silky. Cover loosely with a clean tea towel and leave to rest for 5 mins before using.

Variations:

Using strong plain (bread) flour gives a crustier, more substantial crust to a pie, which is perfect for large or hand raised pies. Hot water crust made with standard plain (all purpose) flour has a more pliable texture and is good for making smaller pies in tins and for use with sweet fillings.

Ingredients

450g (1lb) strong plain or
    standard plain
    (all purpose) flour
1 ½ tsp salt
100g (3 ½ oz) lard or solid
    white vegetable fat
250ml (9fl.oz) water

Flaky Pastry

Ingredients

200g (7oz) strong plain or plain
   (all purpose) flour
Pinch of salt
150g (5oz) half unsalted butter
   and half lard or solid white
   vegetable fat
1 Tbsp fresh lemon juice
100ml (3 ½ fl.oz) cold water

This is the most common of all the flaked pastries and can be used in sweet and savoury cooking. Don't be daunted by the instructions, the method isn't as complicated as it looks. It is best with white flour.

1. Mix together the flour and salt. Put the fat on a plate. Using a small palette knife or round bladed kitchen knife, carefully press to gently soften the fat, and then divide into 4 equal amounts.

2. Using both hands, rub one quarter of the fat into the flour between finger and thumb tips until well blended.

3. Add the lemon juice and sufficient water, stirring with a round bladed knife until the mixture comes together to make a firm, elastic dough.

4. Lightly flour the work surface and roll out the dough into a rectangle 10 x 30cm (4 x 12inch). Arrange another quarter of the fat, in small pieces, evenly over the top two thirds of the dough.

5. Fold the bottom third of the dough up over the middle section (see picture right), and then fold down the top third of the dough on top with the fat inside. Turn the dough round 90° so that the folds are now at the side and gently press the edges together to seal using your rolling pin.

6. Re-roll the dough into the long rectangle as before, and continue the process using another portion of the fat, folding and turning as before. Repeat to use up the last portion of fat, and then roll and fold the dough twice more to thoroughly incorporate the fat.

7. Wrap the pastry loosely in baking parchment and chill for at least 30 mins. After this time, the pastry will be ready to use immediately or wrap well and store in the fridge for up to 3 days.

Rough Puff Pastry

Serves: 500g (1lb 2oz)   Preparation: 30 mins plus chilling

Ingredients

200g (7oz) strong plain or plain
    (all purpose) flour
Pinch of salt
150g (5oz) unsalted butter and
    lard or solid white vegetable
    fat
1 Tbsp fresh lemon juice
100ml (3 ½ fl.oz) cold water

Similar to flaky but simpler to prepare. It does give a slightly more higgledy-piggledy result when baked, but can be used in all recipes where flaky is required, although where an even rise is called for (vol au vents) it is advisable to use flaky. Choose the rough puff method if you find flaky too much of a chore or have less time available.

1. Mix together the flour and salt. Cut the fat into small pieces about 2cm (¾inch) thick and toss into the flour without breaking them up.

2. Add the lemon juice and sufficient water, stirring with a round bladed knife until the mixture comes together to make a fairly stiff dough.

3. Lightly flour the work surface and roll out the dough into a rectangle 10 x 30cm (4 x 12inch).

4. Fold the bottom third of the dough up over the middle section, and then fold down the top third of the dough on top. Turn the dough round 90° so that the folds are now at the side and gently press the edges together to seal using your rolling pin (see picture opposite).

5. Re-roll the dough into the long rectangle as before, and continue the process folding and turning as before. Repeat the rolling and folding 3 more times (5 times in total) until the fat is incorporated.

6. Wrap the pastry loosely in baking parchment and chill for at least 30 mins before using. This will make the pastry easier to handle. After this time, the pastry will be ready to use immediately or wrap well and store in the fridge for up to 3 days.

Puff Pastry

Serves: 525g (1lb 2½oz)   Preparation: 40 mins plus chilling

Ingredients

200g (7oz) strong plain
   or plain flour
Pinch of salt
200g (7oz) piece unsalted butter
1 Tbsp fresh lemon juice
100ml (3 ½ fl.oz) cold water

The richest of all pastries; most even rising, most flaky, most buttery and the crispiest of flaky pastries, but time consuming to make so you may want to save this one for a special occasion. Puff pastry making requires careful preparation and is best made up the day before you want to use it. Puff pastry can be used for sweet or savoury dishes. Readymade puff pastry is widely available fresh and frozen and is probably the most successful of all commercially produced pastries. Puff pastry is best made with white flour and unsalted butter.

Note: if your pastry has been stored in the fridge for a while, allow to stand at room temperature for about 20 mins before baking.

1. Mix together the flour and salt. Using your fingertips, rub 25g (1oz) butter into the flour until well blended.

2. Put the remaining butter on a board. Using a small palette knife or round bladed kitchen knife, carefully press the butter to gently soften it, keeping it one piece, then form into a rectangle about 10cm (4inches) long.

3. Add the lemon juice and sufficient water to the flour, stirring with a round bladed knife until the mixture comes together to make a fairly stiff dough.

4. Lightly flour the work surface and roll out the dough to make a 23cm (9inch) square, and place the piece of butter on one half. Fold over the dough to enclose the butter, and seal the edges using your rolling pin.

5. Turn the dough so that the fold is at the side, and then roll into a rectangle approx. 40cm (34inch) long.

6. Fold the bottom third of the dough up over the middle section, and then fold down the top third of the dough on top and gently press the edges together to seal using your rolling pin. Roll into a rectangle again and repeat the folding and sealing. Wrap the pastry loosely in baking parchment and chill for 30 mins to rest.

7. Put the pastry back down on a lightly floured surface so that the fold is on the side, and continue to roll, fold, seal and rest 4 more times. After this time, the pastry will be ready to use immediately or wrap well and store in the fridge for up to 3 days.

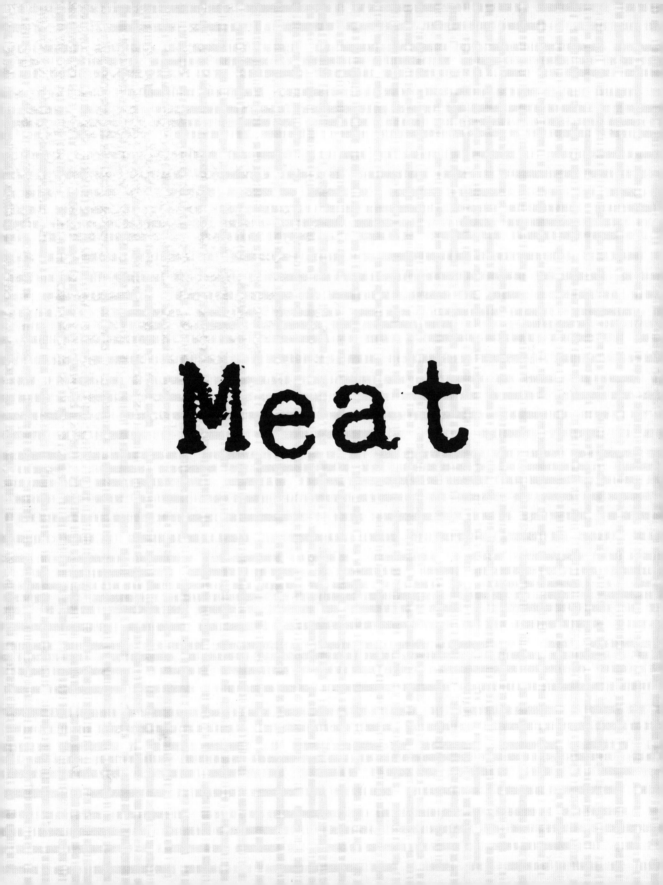

Meat

"Stew and Dumpling" Pie

Serves: 4-6   Preparation: 30 mins plus cooling   Cooking: 3 hours 50 mins

Ingredients

675g (1½ lb) stewing beef such
   as shin, brisket, blade or chuck
   steak, cut into 2cm (¾ inch)
   thick pieces

3 Tbsp plain
   (all purpose) flour

Salt and freshly ground black
   pepper

25g (1oz) dripping or butter

1 Tbsp vegetable oil

1 large onion, peeled and chopped

4 rashers rindless unsmoked
   streaky bacon, chopped

450g (1lb) carrots, peeled and
   sliced

450ml (¾pt) beef stock

2 bay leaves

1 quantity suet crust pastry with
   2 Tbsp chopped parsley and
   3 Tbsp creamed horseradish
   sauce added

1 egg, beaten, to glaze

For a proper, really tasty meat pie you need to make up the filling in advance which requires a bit of forethought and planning. Here, a traditional beef stew is made up and then the next day used as the base for a hearty suet crust topped pie. It makes a great meal served simply with green veg.

1. Put the beef in a bowl. Toss in the flour and season well. Mix together making sure the beef is well coated in the flour.

2. Melt the dripping or butter in a large saucepan until bubbling and fry the beef with the four, stirring, for about 5 mins until browned all over. Using a draining spoon, transfer the beef to a heatproof plate.

3. Reheat the pan juices with the oil and gently fry the onion and bacon for 5 mins until softened, then mix the beef back into the pan along with the carrots, stock and bay leaves.

4. Bring to the boil, stirring occasionally, then cover and simmer very gently for about 2½ hours, or until very tender. Allow to cool and discard the bay leaves. Transfer to a 1.65l (2¾pt) oval pie dish with rim 25 x 18 x 7.5cm (10 x 7 x 3inch). Push a pie funnel in the centre. Cover and chill until required.

5. To make the pie, preheat the oven to 220°C, 200°C fan oven, 425°F, gas 7. Roll out the pastry on a lightly floured surface to just larger than the pie dish. Make a cross in the centre for the pie funnel. Carefully cut some of the excess pastry into thin strips and secure on to the edge of the pie dish with water. Brush with egg. Transfer the rolled out pastry to the top and press down on to the edge using a fork. Brush all over with egg.

6. Put the dish on a baking tray and bake for 10 mins, then reduce the temperature to 190°C, 170°C fan oven, 375°F, gas 5 and cook for a further 50 mins to 1 hour until crisp and golden and the meat is piping hot – cover with foil if the pastry browns too quickly. Serve immediately.

Steak and Kidney Double Crust

Serves: 4   Preparation: 30 mins plus cooling   Cooking: 3 hour 15min

There are several ways you can make up this classic pie, but I always go back to a top and bottom pastry pie for complete deliciousness. Leave out the kidney if you prefer. As with many pies, you need to start this one a few hours before to make sure the filling is completely cold before you assemble your pie.

1. Put the beef and kidney in a bowl. Toss in the flour and season well. Mix together making sure the meat is well coated in the flour.

2. Melt the fat in a large saucepan until bubbling and fry the beef and kidney with the flour and onion, stirring, for about 5 mins until browned all over

3. Add a few slugs of Worcestershire sauce and pour over sufficient cold water to barely cover the meat. Bring to the boil, stirring occasionally, then cover and simmer very gently for about 2½ hours, or until very tender. Allow to cool then cover and chill until required. Remove any fat that sets on the surface.

4. To make the pie, preheat the oven to 200°C, 180°C fan oven, 400°F, gas 6. Roll out the shortcrust pastry on a lightly floured work surface to cover the base of a 24 x 4cm (9½ x 1¾inch) round pie dish with rim. Trim as necessary and spoon the cold meat filling into the pastry case. Brush the edge of the pastry with beaten egg.

5. Roll out the flaky pastry to cover the pie dish. Trim to neaten and pinch the edges of the pastry together to seal. Make a hole in the centre and brush all over with beaten egg. Stand the pie dish on a baking tray and bake in the oven for about 40 mins until richly golden and the filling is piping hot. Best served hot with extra Worcestershire sauce

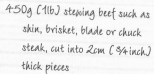

Ingredients

450g (1lb) stewing beef such as shin, brisket, blade or chuck steak, cut into 2cm (¾inch) thick pieces

225g (8oz) ox, pig's or sheep's kidneys, skinned, cored and chopped

3 Tbsp plain (all purpose) flour

Salt and freshly ground black pepper

25g (1oz) dripping, lard or vegetable fat

1 onion, peeled and sliced

Worcestershire sauce to taste

½ quantity shortcrust pastry

½ quantity flaky pastry

1 egg, beaten, to glaze

Pub Grub (Beef and Ale) Pies

Makes: 4 Preparation: 30 mins plus cooling Cooking: 3 hours 20 mins

Ingredients

675g (1 ½ lb) stewing beef such as shin, brisket, blade or chuck steak, cut into 2cm (¾ inch) thick pieces

3 Tbsp plain (all purpose) flour

Salt and freshly ground black pepper

25g (1oz) dripping or butter

1 Tbsp vegetable oil

1 onion, peeled and chopped

4 field or flat mushrooms, peeled and sliced

8 rashers rindless smoked streaky bacon, chopped

450ml (¾ pt) bitter ale or similar

A small bunch fresh thyme, tied with clean string

½ quantity flaky pastry

1 egg, beaten, to glaze

Any self respecting pub will have a pie on their menu, and those specialising in different types of local brews and beers often reflect the fact in their cooking too. The final choice is up to you, but I like "Newcastle Brown" in my pie (plus a little bit more to wash it down!). Cheers!

1. Put the beef in a bowl. Toss in the flour and season well. Mix together making sure the beef is well coated in the flour.

2. Melt the dripping or butter in a large saucepan until bubbling and fry the beef with the flour, stirring, for about 5 mins until browned all over. Using a draining spoon, transfer the beef to a heatproof plate.

3. Reheat the pan juices with the oil and gently fry the onion, mushrooms and bacon for 5 mins until softened, then put the beef back into the pan along with the bitter and thyme.

4. Bring to the boil, stirring occasionally, then cover and simmer very gently for about 2½ hours, or until very tender. Allow to cool and discard the thyme, then transfer to 4 x 300ml (½pt) individual pie dishes. Cover and chill until required.

5. To make up the pies, preheat the oven to 220°C, 200°C fan oven, 425°F, gas 7. Divide the pastry into 4 equal pieces and roll out each piece on a lightly floured surface to just larger than the top of the pie dish. Carefully cut some of the excess pastry into thin strips and secure on to the edge of the pie dishes with water. Brush with egg. Transfer the rolled out pastry to the top, trim and press down on to the edge using a fork.

6. If liked, roll out any leftover trimmings and use pastry cutters to make your chosen design. Stick on top of the pie using beaten egg. Make a hole in the centre and brush the pastry all over with egg.

7. Put the dishes on a large baking tray and bake for 15 mins, then reduce the temperature to 190°C, 170°C fan oven, 375°F, gas 5 and cook for a further 25 mins until risen and golden and the meat is piping hot. Serve immediately.

Variation

If you like a dark, rich flavour choose a stout or Guinness; old fashioned "best bitter" will give you a hoppy, yeasty gravy, while light ales and lagers make a mellower liquor. Use half water and half beer for a lesser yeasty flavour.

Muffin-tin Corned Beef and Bean Pies

Makes: 9 Preparation: 25 mins Cooking: 40 mins

Some pies are best served straight from the oven, but these are fine served cold, ideal for a picnic or packed lunch with tomato ketchup or chutney. No advance filling preparation required either (you can even use up leftovers), so if you fancy a pie in a hurry, here's one to try.

1. Roll out the pastry thinly on a lightly floured surface, and stamp out 9 x 10cm (4inch) rounds using a pastry cutter, re-rolling the pastry as necessary.

2. Carefully press each pastry circle into 7cm (2¾ inch) diameter, 3½ cm (1¼ inch) deep muffin tins. Chill while you make the topping.

3. Preheat the oven to 200°C, 180°C fan oven, 400°F, gas 6. Put the butter or margarine in a bowl and beat in the flour until well blended and forms a rich crumbly mixture. Stir in the grated cheese.

4. Divide the potato between each pastry case. Mash the corned beef with the tomato ketchup and pile on top of the potato, then add a layer of baked beans. Pile the cheesy crumble on top to cover the filling. Bake in the oven for about 40 mins until golden and piping hot. Cool in the tins for 10 mins before serving or transfer to a wire rack to cool completely, then wrap and chill until ready to serve.

Variation
If corned beef's not your thing, you can use any leftover cooked minced or finely chopped meat or chicken in this recipe.

Ingredients

1 quantity wholewheat or spelt shortcrust pastry
50g (2oz) butter or margarine, softened
125g (4 ½ oz) wholewheat or spelt flour
75g (2 ½ oz) mature Cheddar cheese, grated
225g (8oz) cold mashed potato
115g (4oz) corned beef
2 Tbsp tomato ketchup
175g (6oz) canned baked beans in tomato sauce

Scottish "Coo" Pies

Makes: 9 Preparation: 45 mins Cooking: 40 mins

When I moved to Scotland a few years ago, I found myself in "pie heaven". All the local bakeries sell umpteen pastry creations, and meat pies are probably the most popular and famous; this is my version of a classic Scotch beef hand-held pie.

1. Put the minced beef in a bowl and mix in the fat, onion, turnip or swede, salt and plenty of pepper. Divide into 9 portions and form each into a burger shape approx. 8cm (3¼inch) diameter. Set aside.

2. Make up the hot water crust pastry. Keep the remainder of the pastry warm while preparing each of the pies. Set aside one quarter of the pastry and keep covered.

3. Roll out the remaining pastry thinly on a lightly floured work surface, and using a 15cm (6inch) pastry cutter or upturned saucer, stamp out 9 circles, re-rolling the pastry as necessary.

4. Taking one piece of pastry at a time, place a portion of meat in the centre. Bring up the sides of the pastry to enclose the meat, leaving the top oven, and bring the pastry up about 1cm (½inch) higher than the filling. Flatten the bottom and smooth the sides to neaten the shape. Place on a lightly greased baking tray. Repeat to use up the remaining pastry circles and filling.

5. Preheat the oven to 200°C, 180°C fan oven, 400°F, gas 6. Roll out the remaining pastry thinly and cut out 9 x 8cm (3 ¼ inch) circles, re-rolling as necessary. Brush the inside of each pie with beaten egg and push a pastry circle on top of the meat. Pinch the pastry edges together to seal.

Ingredients

500g (1lb2oz) lean Aberdeen Angus beef steak mince (ground beef)

25g (1oz) beef suet or melted butter

1 onion, peeled and finely chopped

150g (5oz) turnip or swede, peeled and grated

1 tsp salt

Freshly ground pepper

1 quantity hot water crust pastry

1 egg, beaten, to glaze

6 . If you like, roll out any pastry trimmings quite thickly and cut out 9 pairs of cow horn shaped pieces. Place on another lightly greased baking tray.

7 . In the top of each pie, make a central slit for steam to escape if you are making undecorated pies, otherwise cut 2 slits either side where the pastry horns can be inserted. Brush the pie tops with egg, and also the pastry horns if made.

8 . Bake the pies for 40 mins until richly golden and the filling is piping hot. The pastry horns will take about 15 mins. Serve the pies hot or cold, and insert a pair of pastry horns in the top if liked. Good with tomato ketchup!

"Eastenders"

Makes: 4   Preparation: 30 mins   Cooking: 40 mins

At the start of my career, I worked on a well known woman's magazine. Our kitchen helper was a lovely lady from East London. One day she brought us in traditional "pie and mash" for lunch. To be truthful, it wasn't my ideal lunch, but for supper, it would have been just perfect. Here's my interpretation, many years on.

1. Preheat the oven to 190°C, 170°C fan oven, 375°F, gas 5. Put the minced beef in a bowl and add 4 Tbsp cold water, then mix in the flour, onion, nutmeg and plenty of seasoning.

2. Set aside one third of the pastry, and divide the remainder into 4 equal pieces. Roll each piece thinly on a lightly floured surface to fit 4 non stick 250ml (9fl.oz) pie dishes with rims – 13½ x 10 x 3cm (5¼ x 6 x 1¼ inch), and line each one, covering the rim as well. Trim as necessary.

3. Divide the filling between each tin, pressing it into the case. Roll out the remaining pastry thinly to make lids to fit inside the pie tin, directly on top of the meat. Lay the lids on top of the meat and press down to fit snugly.

4. Brush the inside of the pastry with egg then fold over the pastry from the rim, pressing with your thumb at intervals to make a "crimped" edge inside the tin. Make a slash in the centre of each, place on a baking tray and brush with milk. Bake in the oven for about 40 mins until golden and the filling is piping hot.

5. Meanwhile, make the liquor. Put the cornflour in a saucepan and gradually blend in half the milk to make a paste. Stir in the remaining milk along with the stock. Heat, stirring, until boiling, and cook for 1 minute until thickened. Remove from the heat and stir in the parsley, colouring if using, and season to taste. Set aside until ready to serve.

Ingredients

350g (12oz) lean minced (ground) beef
25g (1oz) plain (all purpose) flour
1 small onion, peeled and grated
Pinch of ground nutmeg
Salt and freshly ground black pepper
1 quantity fat reduced shortcrust pastry
2 Tbsp whole milk, to glaze

For the "liquor":
2 Tbsp cornflour (cornstarch)
150ml (¼ pt) whole milk
300ml (½ pt) chicken or vegetable stock
6 Tbsp freshly chopped parsley
Green food colouring, optional

6 . Just before serving, reheat the sauce for 2–3 mins. Turn the hot pies out of the tins, break the pastry tops and pour over the liquor. Accompany with mashed potato and mushy peas.

Variation
Standard shortcrust pastry works just as well for this recipe but gives a shorter crust.

Beef and Onion "Clanger"

Serves: 4-6 Preparation: 25 mins plus cooling Cooking: 55min

I remember making a version of this dish in my school home economics class. The dish originates from Bedfordshire in England when it was served up to the workers with meat at one end and fruit at the other – rather like the original Cornish pasties. This all-savoury roly-poly pie uses the traditional suet crust pastry associated with the original recipe.

1. First make the filling. Put the minced beef in a saucepan with the onion and curry powder. Fry gently, stirring, for about 5 mins to brown all over.

2. Remove from the heat, season well and stir in the flour and gradually mix in the stock. Return to the heat, and slowly bring to the boil, stirring until thickened. Reduce the heat, and simmer gently for 5 mins. Set aside to cool completely then stir in the frozen peas and sultanas.

3. To assemble the clanger, preheat the oven to 190°C, 170°C fan oven, 375°F, gas 5. Lightly grease a large baking tray. Make up the suet crust pastry and roll out on a lightly floured surface to make a 30 x 25cm (12 x 10inch) rectangle.

4. Spread with the cold minced beef mixture, leaving a border of about 2cm (¾inch) at the ends of the shorter sides. Brush the ends with beaten egg, and carefully roll up from one of the shorter sides. Press lightly to seal the edge and place seam-side down on the baking tray. Brush all over with beaten egg and bake for about 45 mins until golden brown and piping hot. Best served hot or warm.

Variation

Follow the basic rolling and baking principle for making a baked jam roly poly pudding – you will need 6–8 Tbsp softened strawberry or jam (jelly) to fill the pudding – I prefer to use vegetable suet for sweet dishes. Serve hot with custard.

Ingredients

175g (6oz) lean minced (ground) beef

1 small onion, peeled and finely chopped

2 tsp mild curry powder

Salt and freshly ground black pepper

1 Tbsp plain (all purpose) flour

150ml (¼ pt) beef stock

75g (2 ½ oz) frozen peas

25g (1oz) sultanas

1 quantity suet crust pastry, made up with 4 Tbsp freshly chopped coriander (cilantro)

1 egg, beaten, for glazing

Mini Pasty Bites

Makes: 18 Preparation: 45 mins   Cooking: 40 mins

Ingredients

175g (6oz) peeled potato

115g (4oz) peeled turnip or
swede

1 small onion, peeled and finely
chopped

225g (8oz) chuck steak,
trimmed and finely diced

Salt and freshly ground black
pepper

1 quantity shortcrust pastry

25g (1oz) butter

1 egg, beaten, for glazing

We spent many family holidays in the South West of England when I was growing up with freshly baked homemade pasties on the beach for a picnic. The Cornish pasty is a truly sacred pastry and I won't attempt to replicate it. Instead I'm basing mine on happy memories.

1. Preheat the oven to 200°C, 180°C fan oven, 400°F, gas 6. Lightly grease a large baking tray. Cut the potatoes and swede into thin slices and then cut the slices into short strips. Place in a bowl and mix in the onion, steak and plenty of seasoning.

2. Roll out the pastry thinly on a lightly floured surface. Using a round pastry cutter, stamp out 18 x 10cm (4inch) rounds, re-rolling the pastry as necessary.

3. Divide the filling between the centre of each, and dot with a little butter. Brush the edges of the pastry with egg and fold each over to make a half moon shape. Press the edges together to seal.

4. Stand each pasty on its folded end, seam-side up, and carefully crimp the edges together between your thumb and forefinger – alternatively, keep the pasties on their side and press the edges with a fork.

5. Place on the baking tray and brush all over with egg to glaze and bake for 10 mins. Reduce the temperature to 180°C, 160°C fan oven, 350°F, gas 4, and continue to cook for a further 30 mins until golden and cooked through. Delicious served hot or cold.

Variation

For larger pasties, use a 15cm (6inch) cutter or saucer to make pastry rounds. Fill and fold in the same way. Bake as above, but extend the cooking time by 10–15 mins at the lower temperature.

Dingles

Makes: 4   Preparation: 25 mins plus cooling   Cooking: 1 hour 30 mins

A great name for a pie. Originating from the Dingle region in County Kerry, Ireland, these mutton or lamb pies were sold on market days and made a filling portable lunch for the shepherds of the area. To be traditional use shortcrust pastry, but I like mine made with a flaky pastry.

1. First make the filling. Heat the oil in a saucepan and gently fry the onion, carrot and lamb with the thyme and plenty of seasoning, for 5 mins, stirring, until the lamb is browned all over.

2. Stir in the flour and gradually stir in the stock. Bring to the boil, then simmer gently, half covered, for about 1 hour or until tender. Set aside to cool.

3. For the pies, preheat the oven to 220°C, 200°C fan oven, 425°F, gas 7. Line a large baking tray with baking parchment. Divide the pastry into 2 equal pieces and roll out each on a lightly floured surface to make a 30cm (12inch) square. Using a 15cm (6inch) round cutter or upturned saucer, stamp out 4 circles from each. Discard the trimmings.

4. Divide the filling between 4 circles. Brush the edges with water and place another circle on top. Seal the edges together by pressing with the prongs of a fork.

5. Transfer to the lined baking tray, make a slit in the centre of each and brush with milk. Bake in the oven for about 25 mins until golden and crisp. Best served warm.

Ingredients

1 Tbsp vegetable oil

1 small onion, peeled and finely chopped

1 small carrot, peeled and finely chopped

300g (10oz) lean boneless lamb shoulder, finely chopped

1 Tbsp freshly chopped thyme or 1 tsp dried

Salt and freshly ground black pepper

1 ½ Tbsp plain (all purpose) flour

200ml (7fl.oz) beef or lamb stock

2 Tbsp whole milk, to glaze

1 quantity rough puff pastry or flaky pastry

A Not So Humble Pie

Serves: 4-6   Preparation: 30 mins plus cooling   Cooking: 3 hours 23 mins

Venison has increased in popularity in recent years. Cooked slowly, its lean, melting texture makes a delicious alternative to beef.

1. First make the filling. Put the venison in a bowl and toss in seasoning and flour. Melt the butter in a large saucepan until bubbling and add the meat along with any remaining flour. Cook, stirring, for about 5 mins until browned all over. Remove from the pan using a slotted spoon and transfer to a heatproof plate.

2. Reheat the pan juices with the oil until bubbling, add the onion, carrot and celery to the saucepan and cook, stirring, for 3 mins. Remove from the heat and add the juniper, bay, sage, vinegar and sugar and stir in the wine.

3. Return venison to the saucepan and add the bay leaves, sage, vinegar and sugar. Bring to the boil, reduce to a simmer, cover and cook gently for about 2 hours until tender. Allow to cool, discard the herbs and transfer to a 2.1l (3½pt) oval pie dish with rim – 25½ x 19 x 7cm (10 ¼ x 7½ x 3inch). Push a pie funnel in the centre. Preheat the oven to 220°C, 200°C fan oven, 425°F, gas 7.

4. Roll out the pastry on a lightly floured surface to just larger than the pie dish. Make a hole in the centre for the pie funnel. Carefully cut some of the excess pastry into thin strips and secure on to the edge of the pie dish with water. Brush with egg. Transfer the rolled out pastry to the top, trim and press down on to the edge using a fork.

5. Roll out the pastry trimmings and cut out an antler design. Secure on top of the pie with beaten egg.

6. Put the dish on a baking tray, brush all over with beaten egg and bake for 15 mins, then reduce the temperature to 190°C, 170°C fan oven, 375°F, gas 5 and cook for a further 50 mins to 1 hour until crisp, golden and hot – cover with foil if the pastry browns too quickly. Serve immediately.

Ingredients

- 900g (2lb) boneless shoulder of venison, trimmed and cut into 2.5cm (1inch) pieces
- Salt and freshly ground black pepper
- 4 Tbsp plain (all purpose) flour
- 25g (1oz) butter
- 2 Tbsp sunflower oil
- 1 red onion, peeled and chopped
- 1 large carrot, peeled and chopped
- 1 stick celery, trimmed and chopped
- 2 tsp juniper berries, crushed
- A few sprigs fresh sage tied with clean string
- 2 Tbsp balsamic vinegar
- 2 Tbsp dark brown sugar
- 450ml (¾pt) red wine
- ½ quantity puff pastry
- 1 egg, beaten, to glaze

Venison and Vegetable Filo Layer

Serves: 4 Preparation: 30 mins Cooking: 50 mins

Ingredients

200g (7oz) carrot, peeled and
  grated
200g (7oz) parsnip, peeled and
  grated
Salt and freshly ground black
  pepper
225g (8oz) turnip or swede,
  peeled and grated
Pinch of grated nutmeg
500g (1lb 2oz) minced venison
1 medium leek, trimmed and
  shredded
2 Tbsp freshly chopped rosemary
  or 2 tsp dried
50g (2oz) butter, melted
4 large sheets of filo pastry

If you're calorie counting, filo pastry is a great choice. You don't have to layer up the sheets with melted butter or margarine, beaten egg is a great alternative and gives a crisp, glossy finish. You can use any minced raw meat in this recipe.

1. Preheat the oven to 200°C, 180°C fan oven, 400°F, gas 6. Layer the carrot and parsnip in the bottom of a 30 x 18 x 3cm (12 x 7 x 1 ¼ inch) rimless oval baking dish and season with salt and pepper. Top with the turnip or swede, season well and sprinkle with nutmeg.

2. Mix the venison mince with the leek and plenty of seasoning and spoon evenly over the top of the vegetables. Mix the rosemary with the butter and spoon 2 Tbsp over the venison.

3. Lay the sheets of pastry on the work surface and brush with melted butter, then scrunch up each sheet to make a loose "rosette" shape and arrange on top of the venison, making sure it is completely covered – pull the pastry rosettes apart again if necessary.

4. Stand the dish on a baking tray and brush with any remaining butter. Bake in the oven for about 50 mins, until golden and cooked through – cover with foil if necessary to prevent over browning. Serve hot with freshly cooked vegetables or a crisp salad.

Variation

To use beaten egg instead of butter, mix all the rosemary into the venison mince, and moisten the mixture with 3 Tbsp beef stock. Follow the instructions in step 3 above using beaten egg instead of the rosemary butter.

Ploughman's Lunch

Makes: 8 Preparation: 40 mins   Cooking: 40 mins

Chunky and tasty, these pies are perfect for a picnic lunch, or, cut in halves or quarters, they make a delicious party snack. You can serve them straight out of the oven, but they have more flavour when cooled.

1. Preheat the oven to 200°C, 180°C fan oven, 400°F, gas 6. Put the pork, bacon, onion and pickle in a bowl and mix well. Season with pepper and set aside.

2. Make up the hot water crust pastry. Keep warm, cut off one quarter of the pastry and keep covered separately.

3. Roll out the remaining pastry thinly on a lightly floured surface and cut out 8 x 15cm (6inch) rounds using a pastry cutter or upturned saucer, re-rolling as necessary. Gently press each circle into 10cm (4inch) diameter, 4cm (1½inch) deep rimless pie tins or moulds. Then put a portion of filling in each and pack down well. Sprinkle each with a layer of grated cheese.

4. Roll out the reserved pastry thinly and cut out 8 x 10cm (4inch) rounds, re-rolling as necessary. Brush the inside of the pastry with egg and put a circle on top of each pie. Seal the edges together using the prongs of a fork. Make a hole in the centre of each and brush the tops with egg.

5. Put the pies on a baking tray and bake in the oven for about 40 mins until rich golden brown. Cool for 10 mins, then loosen the edges with a round bladed knife and carefully remove from the tins. Serve hot or transfer to a wire rack to cool completely before serving.

Ingredients

- 400g (14oz) uncooked pork shoulder, minced
- 200g (7oz) rindless smoked streaky bacon, minced
- 1 onion, peeled and finely chopped
- 8 Tbsp sandwich pickle
- Freshly ground black pepper
- 150g (5oz) mature Cheddar cheese, grated
- 1 quantity hot water crust pastry
- 1 egg, beaten, to glaze

Party Slice

Serves: 10-12   Preparation: 50 mins plus cooling   Cooking: 1 hour 30 mins

In days gone by, no self respecting buffet table would have been complete without this classic sliced pie. Nowadays, we've got so many other choices to offer our guests, it's often overlooked. Traditionally made with minced veal, I prefer to use pork or chicken. It does take a while to make, but it's guaranteed to impress.

1. Preheat the oven to 200°C, 180°C fan oven, 400°F, gas 6. Grease the base and sides of a 28 x 10 x 7.5cm (11 x 4 x 3inch) terrine tin. Put the ham, bacon and minced meat in a bowl and mix in the sage, salt, plenty of pepper and nutmeg. Set aside.

2. Cut off one quarter of the pastry and keep warm. Roll out the remaining pastry thinly on a lightly floured surface to form a rectangle approx. 40 x 25cm (16 x 10inch) and gently press into the tin, right to the top. Trim and reserve the excess pastry.

3. Pack one third of the meat into the pastry case and lay the eggs upright and evenly spaced down the centre. Pack the remaining meat mixture around and over the eggs. Brush the inside edge of the pastry with egg.

4. Roll out the reserved pastry, to fit exactly inside the top of the tin and press down on top of the meat. Pinch the two edges of pastry together all round the top to seal. Make a 1cm (½inch) hole in the centre of the lid and place a large piping nozzle, pointed side down in the hole.

5. If liked, roll out the trimmings, cut out your design and use to decorate the top of the pie, securing on the pastry lid using beaten egg.

Ingredients

- 400g (14oz) uncooked smoked gammon, minced
- 115g (4oz) rindless smoked streaky bacon, minced
- 375g (13oz) lean uncooked minced pork, chicken or veal
- 2 Tbsp freshly chopped sage or 2 tsp dried
- 1 ¼ tsp salt
- Freshly ground black pepper
- ½ tsp ground nutmeg
- 1 quantity hot water crust pastry made with strong plain flour
- 4 cold hard boiled eggs, peeled
- 1 egg, beaten, to glaze
- 4 sheets fine leaf gelatine
- Approx. 250ml (9fl.oz) cold good quality weak or low salt chicken stock

6. Put the tin on a baking tray and glaze the top with egg. Bake for 30 mins, then reduce the temperature to 190°C, 170°C fan oven, 375°F, gas 5, and cook for a further 1 hour until richly golden – cover with foil if it browns too quickly. Stand for 15 mins.

7. Meanwhile, cut the gelatine into small pieces and place in a heatproof jug. Add the stock and leave aside to soak for 10 mins. Place the jug over a pan of simmering water until the gelatine has melted. Mix well.

8. Gradually pour the jelly through the nozzle into the hot pie, allowing the jelly to settle after each pour, stopping when the pie ceases to absorb any more. Remove the nozzle and allow to cool then chill overnight. The next day, release the pie from the tin; using a large serrated knife, cut into slices. Best enjoyed at room temperature.

Old Fashioned Egg and Bacon Pie

Serves: 6   Preparation: 35 mins   Cooking: 34 min

Another of my pies from yesteryear. This one reminds me of tea at my Granny's. Use good quality, fresh eggs for the tastiest filling and chunky smoked bacon but you can use unsmoked if you prefer. This pie tastes great cold, but I prefer it when it's been out of the oven for about half an hour, and still warm.

1. Preheat the oven to 200°C, 180°C fan oven, 400°F, gas 6. Roll out two thirds of the pastry on a lightly floured work surface to fit a 24 x 3½cm (9½ x 1 ¼inch) round, 3½cm (1 ¼inch) deep pie tin or dish with rim. Carefully fit the pastry to the dish and rim, neaten the edges and place on a baking tray. Set aside.

2. Put the bacon in a frying pan and dry fry for 3–4 mins until the sealed all over. Drain on kitchen paper. Set aside.

3. Break the eggs into a jug and beat together until well blended. Stir in the cream or milk, chives if using, salt and plenty of black pepper.

4. Roll out the remaining pastry thinly to make a rectangle about 25cm (10inch) long, and cut into 1cm (½inch) wide strips. Interlace the pastry strips on a round piece of baking parchment, pressing them gently together to seal.

5. Put the bacon in the pastry base and pour over the beaten egg mixture. Brush the pastry edge with a little water. Carefully lift the pastry lattice on the paper and flip or slide on top of the pie. Peel away the paper, press the ends of the pastry strips to the edge of the pie dish and trim to neaten.

6. Bake for 15 mins. Reduce the oven temperature to 180°C, 160°C fan oven, 350°F, gas 4 and cook for a further 15 mins until the pastry and egg filling just set. Serve hot or cold accompanied with crisp salad.

Ingredients

¾ quantity of shortcrust pastry
250g (9 oz) thickly sliced, rindless, smoked back bacon, chopped
4 eggs
450ml (¾ pt) single cream or whole milk
2 Tbsp freshly chopped chives, optional
1 tsp salt
Freshly ground black pepper

Mini Pork and Chorizo Picnic Pies

Makes: 12   Preparation: 30 mins   Cooking: 30 mins

Ingredients

100g (3 ½ oz) pork mince
100g (3 ½ oz) chorizo, skinned
      and finely chopped or minced
2 garlic cloves, peeled and crushed
3 Tbsp red pesto
1 ½ tsp smoked paprika
Freshly ground black pepper
½ quantity wholewheat or spelt
      shortcrust pastry
1 egg, beaten, to glaze

Small savoury pies ideal for packed lunch boxes or party food. Use minced chicken instead of pork, or replace the chorizo with minced bacon for a less spicy snack.

1. Preheat the oven to 200°C, 180°C fan oven, 400°F, gas 6. Put the pork and bacon in a bowl and mix in the garlic, pesto and smoked paprika. Season with pepper and set aside.

2. Roll out the pastry thinly on a lightly floured surface. Using a 9cm (3½inch) round pastry cutter, stamp out 9 circles, reserving the trimmings. Gently press each circle into 7cm (2 ¾inch) diameter, 2cm (¾inch) deep bun tins. Put a portion of filling in each and pack down well to just below the pastry rim. Brush the exposed pastry with water.

3. Roll out the trimmings thinly and stamp out 9 x 6cm (2 ¼inch) rounds, re-rolling as necessary. Press a circle of pastry on top of each pie and seal the edges using the prongs of a fork. Make a hole in the centre of each and brush the tops with egg.

4. Bake in the oven for about 30 mins until rich golden brown. Cool for 10 mins, before carefully removing from the tins and transferring to a wire rack. Serve warm or allow to cool completely. Delicious with tangy tomato and chilli chutney

Variation

For an extra rich version of these pies, use the same quantity of double cheese pastry.

Sausage and Apple Plait

Serves: 4   Preparation: 25 mins   Cooking: 40 mins

This is a giant sausage roll with an impressive folded pastry top. Leave out the apple if you prefer.

1. Preheat the oven to 200°C, 180°C fan oven, 400°F, gas 6. Line a large baking tray with baking parchment. Put the sausagemeat in a bowl and mix in the sage and onion. Set aside.

2. On a lightly floured surface, roll out the pastry into a rectangle 30 x 20cm (12 x 8inches) and spread the sausage meat evenly down the centre. Flatten the meat to a depth of 2.5cm (1inch), keeping it 2cm (¾inch) from either short end.

3. Halve and thinly slice the apple, then arrange the slices, overlapping, all over the sausagemeat. Season well.

4. Make 8 slanting cuts in the pastry to within 1cm (½inch) of the filling at 2.5cm (1inch) intervals on either side of the filling. Fold the end pieces of pastry in and round the ends of sausagemeat to cover it.

5. Take a strip from each side and cross over the filling, all down the length of the sausagemeat to give a plaited effect, sealing with a little egg on top.

6. Carefully transfer to the lined baking tray. Brush all over with egg, sprinkle with poppy seeds and bake in the oven for about 40 mins until golden and cooked through. Serve hot or cold in slices, with mustard.

Variations

For a simple sweet "plait", replace the sausagemeat with a combination of fruity mincemeat and grated marzipan (if liked) and pop the apple on top as described above. For more indulgence, use puff pastry. Best served warm with cream.

Ingredients

450g (1lb) good quality pork sausagemeat

3 Tbsp freshly chopped sage or 2 tsp dried

1 small onion, peeled and finely chopped

½ quantity rough puff pastry

1 small pink or red skinned eating apple, cored, halved and thinly sliced

Salt and freshly ground black pepper

1 egg, beaten, to glaze

2 tsp poppy seeds

"Pulled Pork" and Char-grilled Veg Pie

Serves: 4-6   Preparation: 25 mins plus cooling   Cooking: 1 hour

Ingredients

1 each red and yellow peppers,
deseeded and thickly sliced

1 large courgette, trimmed, halved
and sliced diagonally

1 red onion, peeled and cut into
thick slices

2 Tbsp olive oil

1 Tbsp freshly chopped thyme or
1 tsp dried

Salt and freshly ground black
pepper

350g (12oz) cold "pulled pork"
— see below — or other cooked
meat

8 Tbsp sweet tomato chutney

2 tsp smoked paprika

½ quantity rough puff pastry

1 egg, beaten, to glaze

A few small sprigs fresh thyme

A pie based around an American recipe for cooking pork very slowly. It requires some planning if you're starting from scratch, but is a great way to use up leftovers. Slow cooked pork is one of my favourite meats and it retains its succulence on reheating so is perfect for pie making. Serve this simply with coleslaw and salad

1. Preheat the grill to a medium/hot setting. Line the grill pan with foil. Put the vegetables in a bowl and toss in the oil, chopped thyme and seasoning. Spread out evenly in the grill pan. Cook, turning occasionally, for 15 mins until tender and lightly charred. Leave to cool.

2. Preheat the oven to 200°C, 180°C fan oven, 400°F, gas 6. Put the cold vegetables in the bottom of a 22 x 15 x 5cm (8 ¾ x 6 x 2 inch) oblong pie dish with rim. Season well and put the pork on top. Mix the chutney and paprika together and spoon over the top.

3. Roll out the pastry thinly on a lightly floured surface to just larger than the pie dish. Cut some of the excess pastry into thin strips and secure on to the edge of the pie dish with water. Brush with egg. Transfer the rolled out pastry to the top, trim and press down on to the edge using a fork. Put the dish on a baking tray.

4. Make a hole in the centre of the pie and brush all over with egg. Sprinkle with a few sprigs of thyme. Bake in the oven for about 45 mins until risen, golden, and piping hot. Best served hot or warm, with coleslaw and salad.

To make "pulled pork" (serves 4-6)

Put a large roasting tin of water in the bottom of the oven then preheat
the oven to 120°C, 100°C fan oven, 240°F, gas½. Wash and pat dry a
1.5kg (3lb 5oz) boneless pork shoulder joint (with skin on). Remove
any string and rub all over with 2 Tbsp olive oil. Heat a large frying pan
until hot, add the pork, and cook for 5 mins, turning it to seal all over.
Drain and place in a roasting tin. Mix 2 tsp smoked paprika with 2 tsp
dried oregano and plenty of salt and pepper. Rub all over the pork and
cook in the oven for 3 hours. Remove the tray of water, baste the pork
and continue to cook for a further 3 hours at least, basting occasionally,
or until falling apart. Strip away the skin and fat, and "pull" the cooked
pork meat apart into shreds using two forks. Serve hot or cold.

Mutton Pie

Ingredients

2 Tbsp vegetable oil

2 tsp cumins seeds, roasted and
    lightly crushed

2 tsp coriander (cilantro) seeds,
    roasted and lightly crushed

1.5kg (3lb 5oz) mutton or lamb
    shanks, trimmed

25g (1oz) butter

1 onion, peeled and chopped

2 Tbsp plain
    (all purpose) flour

500ml (17fl.oz) chicken stock

450g (1lb) cooked diced potato

225g (8oz) cooked diced carrot

1 quantity suet crust pastry
    made up with 2 tbsp freshly
    chopped rosemary or 2 tsp
    dried

1 egg, beaten, to glaze

Rosemary to garnish

Mutton today it is quite difficult to get hold of and
expensive. It's my favourite meat for flavour but lamb
shanks make a good substitute.

1. Heat the oil in a large saucepan and cook the seeds with the shanks for about 5 mins, turning it in the oil, to seal it all over. Transfer to a heatproof plate using tongs, reserving the cooking juices in the pan.

2. Reheat the juices with the butter until bubbling and cook the onion, stirring, for 5 mins until softened then stir in the flour to make a paste. Gradually stir in the stock and bring to the boil, stirring constantly, and simmer for 5 mins.

3. Return the shanks to the pan, cover with a tight fitting lid and reduce to a gentle simmer. Cook for about 2 hours, turning the shanks occasionally, or until very tender. Reserving the cooking gravy, take the lamb off the bones in chunky pieces and place in a 1.65l (2¾pt) oval pie dish with rim. Mix in the potato and carrot and pour the gravy on top. Leave to cool.

4. Preheat the oven to 220°C, 200°C fan oven, 425°F, gas 7. Push the bones in if using or place a pie funnel in the middle. Roll out the pastry on a lightly floured surface to just larger than the pie dish. Make small crosses in the pastry for the bones or pie funnel. Carefully cut some of the excess pastry into thin strips and secure on to the edge of the pie dish with water. Brush with egg.

5. Transfer the rolled pastry to the top of the dish, trim to neaten and press carefully down on to the edge using your thumb. Cover the bones with foil to prevent them burning. Brush the pastry with egg.

6. Put the dish on a baking tray and bake for 10 mins, then reduce the temperature to 180°C, 160°C fan oven, 350°F, gas 4 and cook for a further 50 mins to 1 hour until golden and the meat is piping hot – cover with foil if the pastry browns too quickly. Garnish with rosemary and serve immediately.

Speha

Makes: 12   Preparation: 30 mins   Cooking: 33min

Middle Eastern food is never far off my radar; I love the fragrant spices used throughout the region. These Lebanese open lamb and tomato pies are made with a special type of pastry dough, but I use filo for my version, and top with pomegranate seeds to add crunch.

1. Preheat the oven to 200°C, 180°C fan oven, 400°F, gas 6. Lightly grease a large baking tray with some of the melted butter. Heat a frying pan until hot then add the pine nuts and stir 2–3 mins until golden brown. Drain on kitchen paper and set aside to cool.

2. Place the onion in a bowl and mix in the garlic, spices, lamb, molasses or lemon juice, chopped tomato and pine nuts. Season well and mix together until well combined. Divide into 12 equal sized pieces and form into round burger shapes approx. 5cm (2inch) diameter.

3. Taking one sheet of filo at a time, brush all over with butter then fold the bottom third up, brush with butter and fold the top third down. Using a 10cm (4inch) cutter, stamp out 3 rounds. Repeat with the other 3 sheets to give you 12 filo rounds in total. Discard the trimmings and brush with butter.

4. Divide the lamb mixture between the circles, then pinch the rounds together at the four 'corners', bringing up the sides to make a case around the filling but leaving the top open.

5. Arrange the pies on the baking tray and bake for 25–30 mins until golden brown. Serve hot or warm, sprinkled with pomegranate seeds.

SUMAC
Sumac is a powdered spice and key ingredient in many Middle Eastern dishes. It has a powerful, tart citrusy flavour; a little goes a long way.

Ingredients

50g (2oz) butter, melted

25g (1oz) pine nuts

1 small red onion, peeled and finely chopped

1 garlic clove, peeled and crushed

½ tsp ground allspice

½ tsp ground sumac — see below

250g (9oz) lean lamb mince

1 tsp pomegranate molasses or 1 Tbsp freshly squeezed lemon juice

1 large ripe tomato, cored and finely chopped

Salt and freshly ground black pepper

4 large sheets filo pastry, at least 30cm (12inch) long

2 Tbsp fresh pomegranate seeds

Churdles

Ingredients

- 75g (2 ½ oz) unsalted butter
- 1 small onion, peeled and finely chopped
- 50g (2oz) smoked rindless streaky bacon, finely chopped
- 175g (6oz) prepared lambs' liver, finely chopped
- 1 Tbsp freshly chopped sage or 1 tsp dried
- Salt and freshly ground black pepper
- 25g (1oz) fresh white breadcrumbs
- 1 quantity shortcrust pastry
- 1 egg, beaten, to glaze

I spent my later school days in West Sussex, and I can honestly say, I never came across a churdle until I started working in London. These traditional yet relatively unknown mitre-shaped pies are unusual in that they have a lambs' liver filling.

1. Melt 25g (1oz) the butter in a frying pan until bubbling then gently fry the onion and bacon for 5 mins to soften but not brown. Add the liver and cook gently, stirring, for 1–2 mins to just seal the liver all over. Remove from the heat and stir in the sage, plenty of seasoning and the breadcrumbs to make a stuffing mixture. Set aside to cool.

2. To make the pies, preheat the oven to 200°C, 180°C fan oven, 400°F, gas 6. Line a large baking tray with baking parchment. Divide the pastry into 2 equal portions and roll out each on a lightly floured surface to form 24cm (9½inch) squares, then cut each into 4.

3. Divide the filling between each square. Cut the remaining butter into 8 small pieces and dot on top of the filling and brush the edges with water. Working on one at a time, bring up the sides, pinching the edges together in the middle to make a mitre-shaped parcel.

4. Transfer the pies to the lined baking tray and brush all over with egg. Bake in the oven for about 20 mins until golden. Best served warm.

Variation

Some recipes mix grated cheese into the filling. If you fancy trying it, add 75g (2½oz) grated mature Cheddar into the cold filling before putting on to the pastry squares.

Poultry

B'stilla

Ingredients

3 prepared squabs or wood
    pigeons, approx. 600g
    (1lb 5oz) weight

A small bunch each of parsley and
    coriander (cilantro)

1 stick cinnamon

Salt and freshly ground black
    pepper

1 onion, peeled and finely chopped

150g (5oz) butter

4 large eggs, beaten

50g (2oz) flaked almonds

50g (2oz) sultanas

4 Tbsp freshly chopped coriander
    (cilantro)

6 large sheets filo pastry, at least
    30cm (12in) long,
    thawed if frozen

2 tsp icing (confectioner's)
    sugar

1½ tsp ground cinnamon

Pronounced "bas-tee-ya", I had this on my very first trip to Morocco, and have enjoyed making my own version ever since. I'm going back to the traditional filling which uses pigeon but you can use 300g (10oz) cooked chicken (brown meat is best) or duck. The sugar dusting sounds a bit weird but it really works.

1. Wash and pat dry the squabs or pigeons and place breast-side down in a saucepan to which they fit snugly side by side. Add the herbs, seasoning, cinnamon, onion and 50g (2oz) butter. Pour over sufficient water to barely cover the pigeons. Bring to the boil, then cover and simmer very gently for 1 hour. Turn off the heat and allow to cool. Drain the birds, reserving the liquid, discard the skin and carefully strip the meat from the bones and set aside.

2. Strain the cooking liquid into another saucepan and bring to the boil. Cook rapidly for about 10 mins to reduce down by half. Remove from the heat and immediately whisk in the eggs, then return to a very low heat and stir for about 10 mins until thickened like a light custard. Season to taste and set aside.

3. Meanwhile, melt 25g (1oz) butter until bubbling and gently fry the almonds for 4–5 mins, stirring, until they turn golden. Drain on kitchen paper and set aside.

4. Preheat the oven to 200°C, 180°C fan oven, 400°F, gas 6. Melt the remaining butter. Brush a 20cm (8in) round spring-form cake tin with butter and cover the base with 2 overlapping sheets of pastry, leaving the edges overhanging the tin. Brush with butter and continue layering with the remaining sheets, brushing each with butter and leaving the edges overhanging, making sure the tin is evenly lined. Put the cooked meat in the bottom of the tin, scatter with almonds, sultanas and chopped coriander. Pour over the egg mixture.

5 . Fold the overhanging pastry over the filling, piece by piece, brushing with butter as you go then brush the top with any remaining butter and place the tin on a baking tray. Cook for 30 mins until crisp and golden, then turn out, upside down, on to a baking tray lined with baking parchment, and return to the oven to cook for a further 10 mins.

6 . Carefully slide on to a warm serving plate. Dust the top with icing sugar, and lay thin strips of baking parchment in a lattice pattern on top. Dust lightly with cinnamon and carefully remove the paper strips. Serve warm .

Golden Chicken Pie

Serves: 6-8   Preparation: 40 mins plus cooling   Cooking: 2 hours 30 mins

Cold pressed rapeseed oil is truly delicious, very golden and nutritious to boot; I'm a complete convert.

1. Place the chicken breast-side down in a saucepan to fit snugly. Add 1 onion, carrot, celery and bay leaves. Pour over sufficient water to barely cover the chicken. Bring to the boil, then cover and simmer very gently for 1½ hours until tender and cooked through. Turn off the heat and cool.

2. Drain the chicken and carrot (strain the cooking liquid and use as stock) and discard the other vegetables and bay leaves. Discard the chicken skin and carefully strip the meat from the bones, cut into bite-sized pieces along with the carrot and put in a large bowl. Cover and chill until required.

3. Meanwhile, chop the remaining onion. Heat the oil until hot and then gently fry the garlic and onion for 7–8 mins until tender and lightly golden. Set aside to cool.

4. To assemble the pie, preheat the oven to 200°C, 180°C fan oven, 400°F, gas 6. Mix the sweetcorn kernels, cream and creamed sweetcorn into the chicken and carrot along with seasoning. Stir in the onion mixture. Spoon into 25 x 20 x 5cm (10 x 8 x 2 inch) pie dish and push a pie funnel in the centre if liked.

5. Roll out the pastry as thinly as possible – it may crack, so simply patch together. Using a 9cm (3½inch) round cutter, stamp out 9 circles, re-rolling as necessary. If using a pie funnel, cut one circle in half. Lightly roll each piece of pastry a little more to make slightly bigger.

6. Arrange the rounds, overlapping, all over the dish – put the 2 halves either side of the pie funnel if using. Stand the dish on a baking tray, brush with beaten egg and sprinkle with cornmeal. Bake in the oven for about 1 hour until golden and piping hot. Serve immediately.

Ingredients

- 1.5kg (3lb 5oz) corn fed oven ready chicken, washed and dried
- 2 onions, peeled
- 1 large carrot, peeled and roughly chopped
- 2 sticks celery, trimmed and roughly chopped
- 2 bay leaves
- 1 Tbsp cold pressed rapeseed oil
- 2 garlic cloves, peeled and crushed
- 250g (9oz) cooked sweetcorn kernels
- 6 Tbsp double cream
- 418g can cream style sweetcorn
- Salt and freshly ground black pepper
- ½ quantity oil pastry, made up using cold pressed rapeseed oil
- 1 egg, beaten, to glaze
- 1 Tbsp fine ground cornmeal

Upper Crust Guinea Fowl and Grape Pie

Serves: 4 Preparation: 30 mins plus cooling Cooking: 1hr

Ingredients

1 oven-ready guinea fowl,
    quartered (or chicken)
Salt and freshly ground black
    pepper
25g (1oz) plain
    (all purpose) flour
25g (1oz) unsalted butter
2 Tbsp olive oil
2 shallots, peeled and finely
    chopped
1 clove garlic, peeled and finely
    chopped
150ml (¼ pt) dry white wine
200ml (7fl.oz) chicken stock
1 bay leaf
4 Tbsp double cream
175g (6oz) seedless green
    grapes, washed
2 Tbsp freshly chopped tarragon
½ quantity puff pastry
1 egg, beaten, to glaze

Based on the retro dish Chicken Veronique this tasty dish should impress your guests, and the puff pastry lid has the "wow" factor alone. No pre-cooking and cooling required, this one's ready to serve immediately.

1. Wash and pat dry the guinea fowl. Season the flour well and dust all over the meat. In a deep frying pan with a lid, melt the butter with the oil until bubbling and then fry the guinea fowl for about 10 mins, turning occasionally, until golden all over. Drain, reserving the pan juices and put on a heatproof plate.

2. Reheat the pan juices and gently fry the shallot and garlic for 5 mins until softened but not browned and then gradually stir in the wine and stock. Add the bay leaf and replace the guinea fowl in the pan. Bring to the boil, cover and simmer gently for about 30 mins. Stir in the cream, grapes and tarragon and continue to cook for a further 5 mins until tender and cooked through. Discard the bay leaf. Transfer to the heatproof serving dish of your choice and keep warm.

3. Meanwhile, preheat the oven to 220°C, 200°C fan oven, 425°F, gas 7. Line a baking tray with baking parchment. On a lightly floured surface, roll out the pastry to make a rectangle approx. 25 x 23cm (10 x 9inches).

4. Carefully transfer the pastry to the tray and score in a diagonal criss-cross design using a sharp knife. Brush with egg. Bake in the oven for 12–15 mins until golden and risen.

5. To serve, carefully transfer the pastry lid to the top of your serving dish and serve up immediately – you may find it easier to put the pastry on a cutting board to divide up the pastry. Accompany the pie with freshly cooked vegetables or crusty bread and crisp salad.

Christmas Cranberry Turkey Pie

Serves: 6-8   Preparation: 40 mins plus cooling   Cooking: 1hr

Here is a great way to use up leftover Christmas meat. This recipe is essentially a pastry case baked, cooled and ready to fill with a tasty chilled filling. If you don't want to make a white sauce, you can use a combination of reduced fat mayonnaise and yogurt.

1. Preheat the oven to 200°C, 180°C fan oven, 400°F, gas 6. Grease and line a 20cm (8inch) diameter, 4cm (1¾inch) deep loose-bottomed cake tin. On a lightly floured surface, roll out the pastry quite thickly to fit the tin and transfer the pastry inside. Trim and reserve the trimmings.

2. Push a circle of baking parchment into the pastry case and fill to three quarters with baking beans or raw pulses or rice. Place the tin on a baking tray and blind bake for 20 mins.

3. Remove the beans or rice and paper and remove the pastry from the tin. Put on a baking tray, prick the base with a fork and brush inside and out with egg. Bake for a further 20 mins until richly golden. Cool on a wire rack.

4. Meanwhile, roll out the trimmings thinly and cut out a 11cm (4 ¼inch) star shape. Place on a lightly greased baking tray, prick lightly with a fork and brush with beaten egg. Bake for 12–15 mins until golden. Transfer to a wire rack to cool.

5. For the filling, melt the butter in a saucepan. Add the flour and cook for 1 minute. Remove from the heat and gradually stir in the milk. Add the bay leaf, cloves and nutmeg. Return to the heat and cook, stirring, until boiling, then simmer for 2 mins. Remove from the heat, stir in the cream, 2 Tbsp parsley and seasoning. Set aside to cool. Discard the bay leaf and cloves.

Ingredients

½ quantity hot water crust
    pastry
1 egg, beaten, to glaze
25g (1oz) butter
25g (1oz) plain
    (all purpose) flour
300ml (½ pt) whole milk
1 bay leaf
4 cloves
Pinch of grated nutmeg
50ml (2fl.oz) double cream
3 Tbsp freshly chopped parsley
Salt and freshly ground black
    pepper
115g (4oz) prepared
    cranberries, thawed if frozen
50g (2oz) caster (superfine)
    sugar
115g (4oz) cooked turkey meat,
    finely chopped or minced
115g (4oz) cooked gammon,
    finely chopped or minced

6 . Put the cranberries in a small saucepan and add 2 Tbsp water. Heat gently until steaming then simmer for about 3 mins until the berries just begin to soften. Remove from the heat and stir in the sugar. Leave to cool.

7 . To assemble the pie, put the pastry case on a serving plate. Put the turkey and ham in a bowl. Mix in the sauce and season to taste. Spoon into the pastry case and top with the cranberry mixture. Either serve immediately at room temperature or chill for an hour before serving. Sprinkle with remaining parsley to garnish.

Cock-A-Leekie Cheesy Pie

Serves: 4-6 Preparation: 35 mins plus cooling Cooking: 55 mins

A tasty dish for cheese lovers, this top-only pie makes a good supper dish or light lunch. Use blue cheese if you prefer and add some finely chopped celery to the leeks for extra savouriness.

1. Melt half the butter in a frying pan until bubbling and stir fry the leeks for 5 mins until just softened. Set aside to cool.

2. Meanwhile, melt the remaining butter in a saucepan, add the flour and cook for 1 minute. Remove from the heat and gradually stir in the milk. Return to the heat and cook, stirring, until boiling point is reach, then simmer for 2 mins. Remove from the heat, stir in the cheese, season to taste, lay a piece of buttered greaseproof paper on the sauce and set aside to cool.

3. To make up the pie, preheat the oven to 200°C, 180°C fan oven, 400°F, gas 6. Put the chicken in a bowl and mix in the cold leek and sauce. Season as necessary and then spoon into a 20cm (8inch) round pie dish with rim, 4cm (1 ¾inch) deep.

4. Roll out the pastry thinly on a lightly floured surface to form an approx. 22cm (8 ¾ inch) circle. Cut the edges off the pastry to neaten and use these pieces to line the edge of the pie dish, securing them on to the dish with water. Cut the remaining pastry into 12–14 strips.

5. Arrange the strips gently on top of the filling in a diagonal criss-cross pattern – 6 or 7 one way and the remaining in the other direction - then interlace the strips. Once in place secure them on to the pastry edge with beaten egg and trim the edge to neaten.

6. Put the pie on a baking tray, brush with egg and bake for 25 mins. Reduce the temperature to 180°C, 160°C fan oven, 350°F, gas 4 and cook for a further 20–25 mins until golden and hot. Serve immediately.

Ingredients

50g (2oz) butter
1 large leeks, trimmed and
  shredded
25g (1oz) plain
  (all purpose) flour
300ml (½ pt) whole milk
150g (5oz) mature Cheddar
  cheese, grated
Salt and freshly ground black
  pepper
300g (10oz) cooked chicken
  meat, cut into bite-sized
  pieces
½ quantity double cheese pastry
1 egg, beaten, to glaze

Topsy-Turvy "Roast Dinner" Pie

Serves: 6 Preparation: 20 mins plus cooling Cooking: 40 mins

I first made this one Boxing Day with the trimmings left over from the previous day's dinner. Everyone enjoyed it and it's now become a family favourite. Of course, it works with any roast dinner leftovers so you can make up your own combinations.

Ingredients

1 Tbsp vegetable oil

6 baby onion or shallots, peeled and halved

4 rashers rindless streaky bacon, chopped

1 Tbsp freshly chopped sage or 1 tsp dried

225g (8oz) cooked chicken, cut into chunky pieces

12 cooked cocktail sausages or pieces of cooked sausage

6 pieces sage and onion stuffing (packet mix or leftover)

Salt and freshly ground black pepper

½ quantity flaky or rough puff pastry

1 egg, beaten, to glaze

Fresh sage to garnish

1. Heat the oil in a 25cm (10inch) round flameproof and ovenproof dish and gently fry the onions and bacon for 5 mins, stirring, until just softened. Remove from the heat, sprinkle with sage and cool for 20 mins.

2. To make up the pie, preheat the oven to 200°C, 180°C fan oven, 400°F, gas 6. Arrange the chicken pieces, sausages and stuffing evenly in the dish and season.

3. Roll out the pastry on a lightly floured surface to a diameter just slightly bigger all round than the dish and place it over the top. Brush with egg and fold over the edges to neaten. Prick lightly with a fork and bake in the oven for about 35 mins until golden and puffed up. Stand for 10 mins, the carefully invert on to a large warmed serving platter. Serve immediately garnished with sage and accompanied with cranberry sauce.

Variations

- Add pieces of cooked roast vegetable the pan if you have some left over. Keep the different ingredients about the same size so that the pastry fits neatly on top.

- For a sweet version, gently fry slices of apple, pear or peach in butter. Scatter with sugar and top with puff pastry. Bake as above. Best served warm with clotted cream or vanilla ice cream.

Pheasant, Parsnip and Redcurrant Puffs

Serves: 4   Preparation: 30 mins   Cooking: 1 hour 10 mins

A special occasion pie that is ideal for an autumnal evening get-together or Sunday lunch. The pastry top is cooked separately so this way of making a pie means you can either serve your filling immediately or reheat it to serve.

1. Wash and pat dry the pheasant pieces, and season all over. Melt the butter in a large saucepan until bubbling and fry the bacon and onion for 5 mins until softened. Add the pheasant and cook, turning in the butter, for about 5 mins until sealed all over, reserving the pan juices. Remove the pheasant from the pan and put on a heatproof plate.

2. Blend the flour into the cooking juices, then the stock and wine. Add the allspice, redcurrant jelly and parsnips. Bring to the boil, stirring, then return the pheasant to the pan and cover. Reduce to a gentle simmer and cook for about 1 hour until tender and cooked through.

3. Meanwhile, make the pastry lids. Preheat the oven to 220°C, 200°C fan oven, 425°F, gas 7. Line a baking tray with baking parchment. On a lightly floured board, roll out the pastry to a 25cm (10inch) square, and divide into 4 equal portions. Score the tops diagonally with a knife and knock up the edges.

4. Transfer the pastry to a lined tray and brush with egg. Bake in the oven for about 20 mins until golden and puffy. Keep warm.

5. To serve, take the pheasant meat off the bones if preferred and spoon portions onto warm serving plates. Sit a pastry puff on top, garnish and serve immediately with vegetables.

Variations

If you want to make the pheasant filling in advance, simply cool, cover and refrigerate for up to 48 hours. Turn into a saucepan, cover and reheat gently for about 40 mins, stirring occasionally, until piping hot.

Ingredients

Salt and freshly ground black
   pepper
2 x 900g (2lb) oven ready
   pheasant, skinned and
   quartered
25g (1oz) butter
4 rashers rindless smoked streaky
   bacon, chopped
1 onion, peeled and chopped
3 Tbsp plain
   (all purpose) flour
450ml (3/4 pt) game or chicken
   stock
150ml (1/4 pt) red wine
1/2 tsp ground allspice
4 Tbsp redcurrant jelly
350g (12oz) parsnips, peeled
   and diced
1/2 quantity puff pastry
1 egg, beaten, to glaze
Redcurrants and parsley to
   garnish

Chicken Pithviers

Ingredients

40g (1½ oz) butter

1 small onion, peeled and chopped

25g (1oz) flaked almonds

50g (2oz) cooked Basmati rice

115g (4oz) cooked chicken, finely chopped

40g (1½ oz) sultanas

1 tsp ground cinnamon

4 Tbsp freshly chopped coriander (cilantro)

Salt and freshly ground black pepper

1 quantity puff pastry

1 egg, beaten, to glaze

Gâteau pithviers is a traditional rich French puff pastry and almond dessert. I thought the idea could work with a savoury filling, and I've put together some ingredients with a hint of Moroccan spice that transforms a sweet into a main course.

1. Preheat the oven to 200°C, 180°C fan oven, 400°F, gas 6. Line a large baking tray with baking parchment. Melt 25g (1oz) the butter in a frying pan until bubbling then gently fry the onion for 5 mins. Add the flaked almonds and continue to cook, stirring, for a further 2–3 mins until the almonds are lightly golden. Cool for 10 mins.

2. Put the rice and chicken in a bowl and mix in the sultanas, cinnamon and coriander. Season well and stir in the oniony almond mixture.

3. Divide the pastry in half, and on a lightly floured surface, roll out each piece of pastry thinly to form a 30cm (12inch) square. Using an upturned saucer or round cutter, cut out 4 x 15cm (6inch) circles from each square.

4. Arrange 4 circles on the lined baking tray, and divide the chicken mixture between each round. Spread the filling to within 2cm (¾inch) from the edge of the pastry. Dot each a piece of the remaining butter.

5. Brush the pastry edge with beaten egg and place another round of pastry on top. Press the top down over the filling, and knock up the edges to seal.

6. Score the tops lightly in a spiral pattern, and brush with egg. Bake for about 30 mins until golden and puffed up. Best served warm.

Variations

For a veggie version, replace the chicken with cooked mushrooms, cashew nuts, almonds or pistachios.

Gram Pastry with Curried Turkey

Serves: 6   Preparation: 40 mins plus cooling   Cooking: 1 hour 20 mins

I love the beany, earthy flavour of chick pea flour;
it's delicious with Indian flavours and bakes to a
lovely golden colour too. It is best mixed with another
flour to make it easier to work with. I use buckwheat
to make the pie completely gluten free but you can use
spelt or other wheat flour if preferred.

Ingredients

Gram flour to dust

1 quantity gluten free pastry,
    made with half gram flour
    and half brown rice flour

2 Tbsp vegetable oil

1 onion, peeled and chopped

2 garlic cloves, peeled and crushed

2 Tbsp mild curry paste

300g (10oz) skinless, boneless
    turkey meat, chopped

400g can chopped tomatoes

75g (2 ½ oz) dried apricots,
    chopped

4 Tbsp freshly chopped coriander
    (cilantro)

Salt and freshly ground black
    pepper

1 egg, beaten to glaze

1. Dust the work surface lightly with gram flour and roll out two thirds of the pastry to fit a 22cm (8 ¾inch) diameter rimless pie dish, 3cm (1 ¼inch) deep. Transfer the pastry to the dish, and press together any cracks – the pastry. Trim to neaten the edges. Wrap the remaining pastry, and chill along with the pastry case for at least 30 mins.

2. Meanwhile, heat the oil in a saucepan and gently fry the onion and garlic for 5 mins. Stir in the curry paste and turkey and cook for a further 15 mins, stirring, until the turkey is sealed all over.

3. Add the chopped tomatoes, bring to the boil, cover and simmer for 15 mins until the turkey is cooked through. Remove from the heat and stir in the apricots. Set aside to cool, then taste and season, and stir in the coriander.

4. To cook the pie, preheat the oven to 200°C, 180°C fan oven, 400°F, gas 6. Lay a sheet of baking parchment inside the pastry case and fill with baking beans or raw pulses or rice. Bake for 10 mins, then carefully remove the beans and parchment. Put the pie dish on a baking tray.

5. Spoon the turkey mixture in to the pastry case. Roll out the remaining pastry as above to fit just inside the rim of the pie dish and place on top on the filling. Make a hole in the centre and brush with egg.

6. Bake in the oven for about 35 mins until golden and firm. Best served warm, straight from the dish with crisp salad.

Duck and Orange Filo Bites

Ingredients

3 large sheets of filo pastry

75g (2 ½ oz) butter, melted

100g (3 ½ oz) duck pâté

125g (4 ½ oz) cooked duck
   meat, chopped

2cm (¾ inch) piece root ginger,
   peeled and finely chopped

4 tsp dark soy sauce

125g (4 ½ oz) marmalade

1 Tbsp freshly chopped chives

Fine strips of orange zest to
   garnish

Paper thin filo pastry is the ideal choice to wrap around savoury or sweet fillings. Best served warm while the pastry is crisp and buttery.

1. Line a large baking tray with baking parchment. Lay the sheets of filo on top of each other on the work surface in front of you and cut into 12 squarish pieces. Cover with damp kitchen paper.

2. Taking one square at a time, brush with butter then lay another square on top at a slightly different angle. Brush again and repeat with one more square to make a 6 pointed star-shape. Keep covered while preparing the remaining squares to make 12 pastry stars.

3. Brush each star with butter. Divide the pâté, duck meat and ginger between the pastries and form into a mound in the centre.

4. Working on one at a time, bring up all the corners up around the filling, scrunching the pastry together round the filling to make a tightly scrunched but open bundle. Place on the baking tray lined with baking parchment. Once you have finished all 12 you can either cover and chill them for up to 24 hours or cook them straight away.

5. To bake, preheat the oven to 200°C, 180°C fan oven, 400°F, gas 6. Drizzle each with a little soy sauce and top with a small spoonful of marmalade. Brush the pastries with any remaining butter and bake for about 15 mins until crisp and golden. Sprinkle with chopped chives and orange zest. Best served warm.

TIP: You can freeze these pastries, uncooked, for longer keeping. Follow the recipe to the end of step 4 then pack side by side in a rigid freezerproof container and seal. Label and freeze for up to 3 months. Cook from frozen, as above, but allow an extra 5-10 mins to ensure they are thoroughly heated.

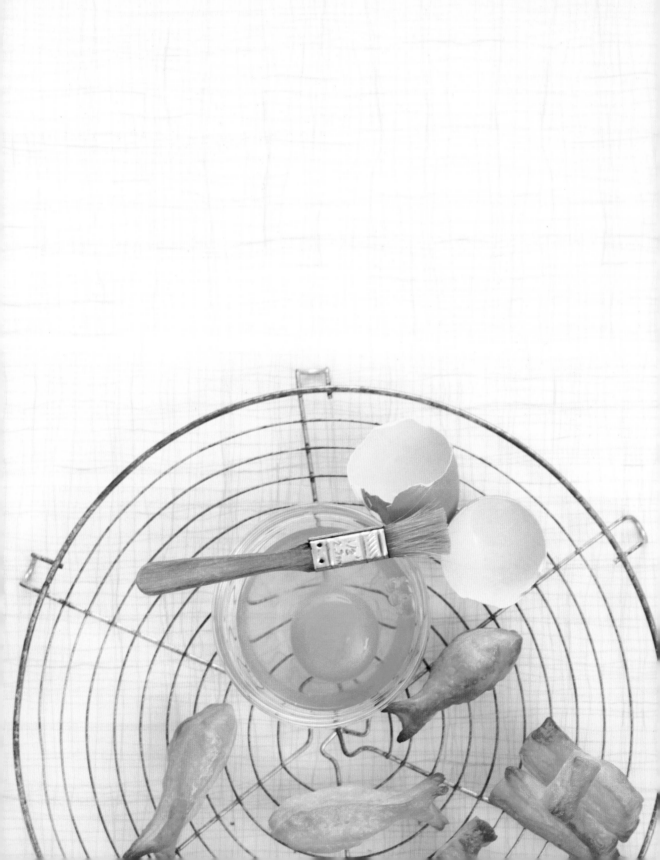

Fish

Smoked Fish, Rice and Pea Handfuls

Makes: 4   Preparation: 40 mins plus chilling and cooling   Cooking: 45 mins

Ingredients

Gluten free flour to dust

1 quantity gluten free shortcrust
    pastry or standard
    shortcrust pastry

250g (9oz) smoked haddock
    fillet

1 bay leaf

1 Tbsp mild curry paste

3 eggs

150ml (¼ pt) whole milk

Salt and freshly ground black
    pepper

4 Tbsp freshly chopped coriander
    (cilantro)

100g (3½ oz) cooked Basmati
    rice

100g (3½ oz) cooked peas

My inspiration for these comes from my love of kedgeree.

1. Preheat the oven to 200°C, 180°C fan oven, 400°F, gas 6. Dust the work surface lightly with gluten free flour, set aside one third of the pastry for the fishy lids. Divide remaining pastry into four and roll out to fit four 10cm (4inch) round rimless non stick pie dishes, approx. 3cm (1¼inch) deep.

2. Transfer the pastry to the tins, and press together any cracks – the pastry is quite crumbly to work with. Trim to neaten the edges and mix the trimmings into the reserved pastry. Chill the reserved pastry until required, and the lined tins for at least 30 mins.

3. Line the pastry with circles of baking parchment and fill with baking beans or raw pulses or rice. Put the tins on a baking tray and bake for 10 mins. Carefully remove the beans or rice, and discard the parchment. Prick the bases all over with a fork and return to the oven for 5 mins to "set" the pastry. Leave to cool.

4. Meanwhile, put the haddock in a frying pan with a lid, add the bay leaf and just cover with water. Bring to the boil, cover and simmer very gently for 5 mins only. Leave to cool in the liquid; then drain, flake the fish and discard the skin and bay leaf.

5. Put the curry paste in a bowl and whisk in 2 eggs, the milk and seasoning until well blended. Stir in the coriander, rice, peas and cooked fish.

6. To bake, reduce the oven temperature to 190°C, 170°C fan oven, 375°F, gas 5. Roll out the reserved pastry thinly and using a 9cm (3 ¾inch) long fish shaped cutter or template stamp out 12 fish shapes, re-rolling as necessary.

7. Divide the fish filling between the pastry cases. Arrange pastry fishes on top and brush with egg. Bake in the oven for about 30 mins until set. Stand for 10 mins before removing from tins. Delicious served warm or cold.

Smoky Salmon Turnover

Serves: 4   Preparation: 30 mins   Cooking: 50 min

I'd never come across hot smoked salmon until I moved to Scotland. Now it is widely available and is succulent and delicious hot or cold. You can use standard smoked salmon if unavailable or cooked smoked haddock or mackerel or cooked prawns are good too.

1. First make a parsley sauce. Melt the butter in a saucepan, add the flour and cook for 1 minute. Remove from the heat and gradually stir in the milk. Return to the heat and cook, stirring, until boiling point then simmer for 2 mins. Remove from the heat, stir in the spring onions and set aside to cool; then stir in the salmon and plenty of seasoning.

2. Preheat the oven to 190°C, 170°C fan oven, 375°F, gas 5. Line a baking tray with baking parchment. Make up the suet crust pastry and roll out on a lightly floured surface to make a 30cm (12inch) diameter circle.

3. Spoon the fish and egg mixture on one half, leaving a border of about 2cm (¾inch). Brush the border with beaten egg, and carefully fold over the other half. Press lightly to seal the edge, then crimp the edge and transfer to the lined baking tray. Using a sharp knife, lightly slash the top.

4. Brush all over with beaten egg and bake for 40–45 mins until golden brown and piping hot. Best served hot, sprinkled with chives, accompanied with rocket salad and lemon wedges.

Variations

Replace the salmon with smoked ham or chicken, or cooked smoked bacon. For a lighter dish, leave out the cheese.

Ingredients

25g (1oz) butter
25g (1oz) plain
   (all purpose) flour
300ml (½ pt) whole milk
1 bunch spring onions (scallions),
   trimmed and chopped
350g (12oz) hot smoked
   salmon, skinned and flaked
Salt and freshly ground black
   pepper
1 quantity suet crust pastry,
   made with vegetable suet and
   50g (2oz) freshly grated
   Parmesan cheese and 4 Tbsp
   freshly chopped chives added
1 egg, beaten, to glaze
Chopped chives to garnish

Salmon, Spinach and Wild Rice Spelt Bake

Serves: 6 Preparation: 40 mins plus cooling Cooking: 55 mins

Ingredients

1 quantity shortcrust pastry,
  made using wholewheat spelt
  flour

225g (8oz) baby spinach leaves,
  trimmed

100g (3 ½ oz) rocket

1 large leek, trimmed, rinsed and
  finely sliced

200ml (7fl.oz) double cream

¼ tsp grated nutmeg

Salt and freshly ground black
  pepper

300g (10oz) salmon fillet

115g (4oz) cooked wild rice

1 egg, beaten, to glaze

Very simple flavours come together in a light wholewheat pastry crust for this pie. Wild rice gives a slight nuttiness to the mixture but brown rice works just as well. Use a traditional wheat flour or plain white flour shortcrust pastry if preferred.

1. Preheat the oven to 200°C, 180°C fan oven, 400°F, gas 6. Roll out two thirds of the pastry on a lightly floured surface to fit a 22cm (8 ¾inch) diameter rimless pie dish, 3cm (1¼inch) deep.

2. Transfer the pastry to the dish. Trim to neaten the edges and mix the trimmings into the remaining pastry. Chill the reserved pastry until required.

3. Line the pastry with a circle of baking parchment and fill with baking beans or raw pulses or rice. Put the dish on a baking tray and bake for 10 mins. Carefully remove the beans or rice, and discard the parchment. Prick the base all over with a fork and return to the oven for 5 mins to "set" the pastry. Leave to cool.

4. Meanwhile, rinse the spinach and rocket leaves and pack into a large saucepan while still wet. Stir in the leeks, cover and cook over a medium heat for 6–7 mins, turning occasionally, until just wilted. Drain well through a sieve or colander, pressing the vegetables against the sides to extract as much water as possible. Leave aside to cool, then blot with kitchen paper, put in a bowl and mix in the cream, nutmeg and plenty of seasoning. Set aside.

5. Put the salmon in a frying pan with a lid. Barely cover with water, bring to the boil, cover and simmer very gently for 5 mins only. Allow to cool in the liquid then drain, flake the fish away from the skin and discard the skin.

6. Put the rice and salmon into the bottom of the pastry case. Top with the spinach mixture. Roll out the remaining pastry to fit the top of the pie dish.

7. Stamp out 2 small fish shapes using a cutter or template and put the pastry circle over the spinach. Press gently to seal the edges together. Brush with egg and stick the cut out pastry fishes on top to decorate. Brush with more egg and stand the pie on a baking tray. Bake for 40 mins until lightly golden and the filling piping hot. Serve hot or cold. well through a sieve or colander, pressing the vegetables against the sides to extract as much water as possible. Leave aside to cool, then blot with kitchen paper, put in a bowl and mix in the cream, nutmeg and plenty of seasoning. Set aside.

Smoked Salmon and Asparagus Envelopes

Makes: 4   Preparation: 30 mins Cooking: 20 mins

Fine asparagus works best for this recipe, but if you have the thicker stems, cut them in half lengthways. I use smoked salmon but you can replace with wafer thin slices of Parma ham or bacon rashers, or add a bit more asparagus without the fish for a vegetarian version.

1. Preheat the oven to 220°C, 200°C fan oven, 425°F, gas 7. Line a large baking tray with baking parchment. Roll out the pastry on a lightly floured surface to a 30cm (12in) square, and cut into four smaller squares.

2. Mix the soft cheese with the herbs and carefully spread over each pastry square to within 2cm (¾inch) of the edge. Lay slices of smoked salmon diagonally across the pastry squares, corner to corner.

3. Trim the asparagus to 18cm (7in) lengths. Divide into 4 bundles of 6, and lay on the pastry square in a diagonal. Season with black pepper, and brush the pastry edge with beaten egg.

4. Bring up two opposite sides of pastry and overlap them on top. Press together on top to seal. Transfer to the baking tray, and brush the asparagus with oil. Brush the pastry with egg and bake in the oven for about 20 mins until golden and tender. Best served warm.

Ingredients

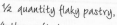

½ quantity flaky pastry,
4 tbsp soft cheese
2 Tbsp freshly chopped dill
2 Tbsp freshly chopped chives
200g (7oz) thinly sliced
   smoked salmon
24 fine asparagus spears
Freshly ground black pepper
1 egg, beaten
1 tsp olive oil

Vol au Vents Fruits de Mere

Makes: 4   Preparation: 25 mins Cooking: 25 mins

Ingredients

1 quantity puff pastry
1 egg, beaten, to glaze
2 Tbsp extra virgin olive oil
2 Tbsp lemon juice
2 Tbsp capers in brine, rinsed
1 tsp caster (superfine) sugar
350g (12oz) assorted cooked
   and prepared shellfish
4 tsp freshly chopped dill
Salt and freshly ground black
   pepper
4 Tbsp olive oil mayonnaise
Fresh dill to garnish

These impressive pastries definitely have the "wow" factor, and are well worth taking time over and the extra effort of making your own puff pastry. Shellfish makes the perfect filling for buttery, flaky pastry; use all prawns or flakes of cooked salmon as an alternative if preferred.

1. Preheat the oven to 230°C, 210°C fan oven, 450°F, gas 8. Lightly grease a baking tray. Roll out the pastry on a lightly floured surface to form a 20cm (8inch) square, about 1cm (½inch) thick. Using a 10cm (4inch) plain pastry cutter, stamp out 4 rounds and place on the baking tray.

2. Cut part the way through the centre of each using a 7cm (3inch) round cutter – this will form the lid. Brush the tops with beaten egg and bake for 20 mins until risen and golden brown.

3. Carefully remove the inner circles of pastry and reserve as lids. Scoop out and discard the soft pastry from inside to leave crisp pastry shells. Cool the cases on a wire rack.

4. Preheat the oven to 190°C, 170°C fan oven, 375°F, gas 5. Put the cases on a baking tray and put back in the oven for 5 mins until hot.

5. Meanwhile, prepare the filling. Put the oil, juice, capers and sugar in a small saucepan and heat very gently until hot (do not boil). Put the shellfish in a heatproof bowl and toss in the dill and seasoning, then mix in the hot dressing.

6. Spoon 1 Tbsp mayonnaise into each vol au vent case. Divide some of the warm shellfish between the cases. Sit the lids back on top, garnish and serve immediately with the remaining shellfish on the side.

Variations

If you prefer a cold filling, simply mix the filling ingredients together and either put into cold pastry cases or reheat the cases as above. For party-sized vol au vents or *bouchées*, roll the pastry as above and use a 5cm (2inch) pastry cutter and cut out 16 rounds. Make the lid using a 2.5cm (1inch) cutter. Bake for about 15 mins then fill with a finely chopped combination of your favourite ingredients.

Mussel, Cockle and Bacon "Pot" Pies

Makes: 4   Preparation: 25 mins plus cooling   Cooking: 30 min

Ingredients

15g (½ oz) butter

4 rindless rashers smoked streaky
   bacon, finely chopped

2 garlic cloves, crushed

1 small onion, finely chopped

150ml (¼ pt) dry white wine

150ml (¼ pt) fish stock

150ml (¼ pt) double cream

4 Tbsp freshly chopped parsley

Salt and freshly ground black
   pepper

450g (1lb) cooked shelled
   mussels

200g (7oz) cooked cockles

½ quantity puff, flaky or rough
   puff pastry

1 egg, beaten, to glaze

These pretty little pies can be made in any small round basin as long as it's ovenproof. They make generous starters or are ideal for lunch or a light supper, and don't forget the spoons for eating the creamy liquor left in the bottom!

1. Melt the butter in a small saucepan and fry the bacon, garlic and onion for 5 mins, stirring, until softened. Pour over the wine, bring to the boil and simmer gently for about 5 mins to reduce down by half. Allow to cool then stir in the stock, cream, parsley and season to taste.

2. Wash and pat dry the mussels and cockles then divide between 4 x 300ml (½pt), 10cm (4inch) diameter ovenproof basins or small enamel pans – use pie birds if liked. Cover and chill until required.

3. When ready to bake, preheat the oven to 220°C, 200°C fan oven, 425°F, gas 7. Divide the pastry into 4 equal pieces and roll out each piece on a lightly floured surface to 2cm (¾inch) larger all round than the basins. Make a small cross in the centre of each.

4. Spoon the garlic and bacon stock over the seafish and brush the outside top edge of the basins with water. Transfer the rolled out pastry circles on top, pressing down to make a good seal over the edge of the basins.

5. Put the basins on a baking tray and brush the pastry tops with egg. Bake for about 20 mins until risen and golden and the filling is piping hot. Serve immediately with crusty bread to mop up the juices.

Variations

If you don't fancy mussels, use cooked prawns or a selection of shellfish. Cooked white fish or salmon also makes a good filling.

Sardine and Tomato Pastries

Makes: 10 Preparation: 45 mins plus cooling Cooking: 25 mins

If you don't have a fish-shaped pastry cutter, make a simple shape on a piece of thick cardboard and use it as a template. These little fishes look lovely "swimming" on a large platter, perfect for a buffet or cocktail party. Use canned fish if preferred.

1. Line a large baking tray with baking parchment. Preheat the grill to a medium/hot setting. Wash and pat dry the fish. Line the grill pan with foil and arrange the sardines on top, skin-side down. Season and cook for about 5 mins until cooked through. Flake the fish into a heatproof bowl. Allow to cool, then mix in the oil, garlic, tomato, parsley and chutney.

2. Divide the pastry in half and roll out each half thinly on a lightly floured surface to 30cm (12inch) squares. Cut out 8 x 16 x 6cm (15½ x 2½ inch) long fish shapes from each square. Gather up the trimmings, re-roll and cut out a further 2 fishes – use these for pastry bases. You should have 20 fishes in total.

3. Divide the filling between 10 fishes and evenly spread down the centre of each. Brush the edges with egg. Carefully place another fish on top and press round the edge to seal. Knock up the edges.

4. If liked, make scale patterns on the pastry using a small sharp knife, and make a small hole in each for an eye. Cover and chill until ready to bake.

5. To bake, preheat the oven to 220°C, 200°C fan oven, 425°F, gas 7. Remove the covering and brush the pastry fishes with beaten egg. Bake in the oven for about 20 mins until golden and puffed up. Best served warm with lemon wedges, a crisp salad and tomato chutney.

Ingredients

200g (7oz) fresh sardine fillets
Salt and freshly ground black pepper
1 Tbsp olive oil
2 garlic cloves, peeled and finely chopped
1 ripe tomato, finely chopped
2 Tbsp freshly chopped parsley
3 Tbsp sweet tomato chutney (plus extra to serve)
1 quantity flaky pastry
1 egg, beaten to glaze

Anchovy, Olive and Caper Mille Feuille

Makes: 6 Preparation: 30 mins plus cooling Cooking: 15 mins

Ingredients

½ quantity puff pastry

1 egg, beaten

50g can anchovies, drained and
chopped

2 spring onions (scallions),
trimmed and finely chopped

25g (1oz) pitted black olives,
finely chopped

2 Tbsp freshly chopped parsley

2 Tbsp freshly chopped tarragon

2 Tbsp freshly chopped coriander
(cilantro)

2 Tbsp capers in brine, drained
and rinsed

Freshly ground black pepper

6 Tbsp crème fraîche

These French pastries are most usually made and filled with fresh cream and fruit; the name means "thousands of leaves" and refers to the flaky layers of pastry. You can make them in different sizes for serving as a starter or canapé.

1. Preheat the oven to 220°C, 200°C fan oven, 425°F, gas 7. Line a baking tray with baking parchment. On a lightly floured surface, roll out the pastry to make a rectangle approx. 25 x 23cm (10 x 9inches).

2. Carefully transfer the pastry to the tray and prick all over with a fork. Brush lightly with egg. Bake in the oven for 12–15 mins until golden and risen. Leave to cool on the tray.

3. Carefully transfer the pastry to a board and using a large sharp knife, cut in half lengthways, and then cut each half into 6 equal slices.

4. When ready to serve, mix the remaining ingredients together except the crème fraîche. Spread 6 unglazed pastry slices with crème fraîche and sprinkle over the anchovy mixture. Top with the remaining pastry, glazed side up, and serve immediately.

Variations

For a sweet version, sprinkle the top of the pastry with 1 Tbsp caster sugar before baking. Thinly slice 6 strawberries and lightly whip 150ml (¼pt) double cream. Sandwich 2 pieces of pastry together, sugar side up, with whipped cream, sliced strawberries and a little strawberry jam (jelly) . Serve immediately.

Prawn Pizza Pie

Serves: 4-6   Preparation: 30 mins plus cooling   Cooking: 35 min

An extra rich treat for pizza lovers. I think it was in an American diner that I first had a pizza pie, filled with meat balls and tomato sauce. This fishy version can be easily adapted to take your favourite filling. Use traditional shortcrust or gluten free pastry if preferred.

1. Heat the oil in a saucepan and gently fry the garlic for 1–2 mins until softened but not brown. Add the tomatoes and sugar, bring to the boil and simmer gently for 7–8 mins until thickened. Stir in the olives and leave to cool. Season to taste.

2. Preheat the oven to 200°C, 180°C fan oven, 400°F, gas 6. Roll out the pastry on a lightly floured surface to fit a 23cm (9inch) diameter, 3cm (1 ¼inch) deep rimless pie plate or tin. Trim to neaten the edge, then prick all over with a fork.

3. Put the plate on a baking tray and bake for about 15 mins until lightly cooked. Set aside to cool.

4. When ready to serve, mix the prawns into the tomato sauce and spread all over the pastry case. Arrange the sliced cheese on top. Bake in the oven for about 25 mins until lightly golden and heated through. Best served hot, sprinkled with fresh basil, whole black olives and capers.

Variations

For a vegetarian version, leave out the prawns and anchovies, and replace with 225g (8oz) lightly cooked sliced mushrooms. Sprinkle with 2 Tbsp freshly grated parmesan cheese just before baking.

Ingredients

1 Tbsp olive oil

2 garlic cloves, crushed

400g can chopped tomatoes

1 tsp caster (superfine) sugar

50g (2oz) pitted black olives, chopped

Salt and freshly ground black pepper

½ quantity oil pastry, made with olive oil

175g (6oz) cooked large peeled prawns

150g (5oz) ball mozzarella cheese, drained and sliced

25g (1oz) whole pitted black olives

1 Tbsp capers in brine, drained and rinsed

A few fresh basil leaves

Tunisian Tuna Bricks

Makes: 4   Preparation: 30 mins   Cooking: 9 mins

Ingredients

185g can tuna in olive oil, drained
  and flaked
1-2 tsp harissa paste, see below
Salt and freshly ground black
  pepper
1 red onion, finely sliced
1 red chilli, deseeded and finely
  sliced, optional
4 Tbsp freshly chopped coriander
  (cilantro)
4 square sheets brick or filo
  pastry sheets
4 eggs
Vegetable oil for shallow frying
Lemon wedges to serve

I wasn't sure about this Tunisian street food snack when I first came across it. But I did enjoy it very much! Brick pastry is wafer thin and very crispy. Filo pastry makes an easier-to-obtain alternative.

1. In a bowl, flake the tuna and mix with harissa paste to taste, and season. In another bowl mix the onion, chilli, if using, and coriander together, and stir half into the tuna.

2. To use brick pastry, lay one sheet at a time on the work surface, shiny side down, and put one quarter of the tuna mixture in a rectangular mound in the centre of the pastry. Make a slight indent in the centre. Brush the pastry with water.

3. Carefully break an egg over a small bowl to drain off about half the egg white, then put the rest of the egg on to the tuna. Fold over all the sides of the pastry, pressing well to seal to end up with a folded parcel about 12 x 8cm (5 x 3½inch). Repeat with the remaining pastry sheets and filling. If using filo pastry, fold each sheet to make a square and follow the same instructions.

4. To cook, pour sufficient oil into a large frying pan to a depth of 1cm (½inch) and heat for over a medium heat for about 1 minute until hot. Carefully lower 2 bricks into the oil, folded side up and cook for 1 – 1½ mins until lightly crisp and golden. Carefully turn over (the pastry is thin so take care not to tear it) and cook for a further 2–3 mins until richly brown and crisp. Remove from the oil with a slotted spoon, drain and keep warm while you cook the other bricks. Serve immediately with lemon wedges, accompanied with remaining onion salad.

Harissa paste:
A fiery hot chilli-based paste from North Africa, flavoured with cumin, mint and garlic. Use a chilli paste or sauce if unavailable.

Vegetables

Macaroni Cheese Pies

Makes: 6   Preparation: 40 mins plus cooling   Cooking: 43 mins

A favourite hearty snack hailing from Scotland. Every baker has their own version of these pies and they are delicious served straight out of the oven with tomato ketchup and chips! I use pie rings to make them but you can just as easily shape your own free-form cases.

1. Melt the butter in a saucepan and stir in the flour. Cook for 1 minute. Remove from the heat and gradually stir in the milk. Return to the heat and cook, stirring, until the mixture comes to the boil and thickens. Cook for a further 1 minutes then remove from the heat and stir in 100g (3½oz) grated cheese. Cover the surface with a piece of greaseproof paper and set aside.

2. Meanwhile, bring a large saucepan of lightly salted water to the boil. Add the macaroni and cook for 7–8 mins until just tender. Drain well, return to the saucepan and stir the cheese sauce into the macaroni. Season to taste, cover as above and leave to cool.

3. Preheat the oven to 200°C, 180°C fan oven, 400°F, gas 6. Make up the hot water crust pastry. Roll out the pastry thinly on a lightly floured surface to enable you to cut out 6 x 11.5cm (4½inch) rounds using a pastry cutter. Gently press each circle into 9cm (3¾inch) diameter, 4cm (1½inch) deep pastry rings or tins. Transfer the pastry rings to a baking tray.

4. Spoon a portion of the cold macaroni cheese filling into each and pack down well, but make sure the macaroni comes to just below the pastry edge. Sprinkle with the remaining grated cheese.

5. Bake in the oven for about 35 mins until rich golden brown. Loosen the edges with a round bladed knife and cool for 5 mins, before removing the pies. Best served hot or warm with tomato ketchup.

Ingredients

25g (1oz) butter
25g (1oz) plain (all purpose) flour
300ml (½ pt) whole milk
200g (7oz) mature Cheddar cheese, grated
Salt and freshly ground black pepper
150g (5oz) macaroni
½ quantity hot water crust pastry

A Very Virtuous Vegetable Pie

Serves: 4   Preparation: 30 mins   Cooking: 48 mins

Ingredients

450g (1lb) sweet potatoes,
 peeled and cut into small
 chunks

Salt and freshly ground black
 pepper

4 Tbsp vegetable stock

250g (9oz) courgette
 (zucchini), trimmed and
 coarsely grated

225g (8oz) leek, trimmed and
 finely shredded

2 garlic cloves, peeled and crushed

2 tsp ground cumin

250g (9oz) cooked peeled
 beetroot, coarsely grated

350g (12oz) cooked sweetcorn
 kernels

4 large sheets filo pastry

1 egg, beaten

2 tsp cumin seeds, lightly crushed

Compared with most other pastries, filo has quite a low fat content, so if you leave out the butter and use beaten egg instead, you can enjoy a slice of comfort every now and then without feeling too guilty.

1. Put the potatoes in a saucepan, cover with water and add a pinch of salt. Bring to the boil and cook for 7–8 mins until tender. Drain well then return to the saucepan and mash smoothly. Leave to cool.

2. Meanwhile, heat the stock in a frying pan until steaming then add the courgette, leek, garlic and ground cumin and cook, stirring, for 3–4 mins until slightly tender. Leave to cool.

3. When ready to assemble, preheat the oven to 200°C, 180°C fan oven, 400°F, gas 6. Spoon the beetroot into the bottom of a 30 x 18 x 3cm (12 x 7 x 1 ¼ inch) baking dish. Season well, then top with sweetcorn.

4. Spoon over the courgette and leek mixture allowing the cooking liquid to seep through the layers. Season again, then carefully spread the sweet potato mash over the top.

5. Lay the sheets of pastry on the work surface and brush with egg, then scrunch up each sheet to make a loose "rosette" shape and arrange on top of the potato, making sure it is completely covered – pull the pastry rosettes apart again if necessary.

6. Stand the dish on a baking tray, brush with egg and sprinkle with cumin seeds. Bake in the oven for about 40 mins, until golden and cooked through – cover with foil if necessary to prevent over browning. Serve hot with a crisp salad.

Mediterranean Butterbean and Vegetable Pie

Serves: 6 Preparation: 40 mins plus cooling Cooking: 1 hour

Most pies from eastern Mediterranean regions use filo pastry. I have combined a classic bean dish from the region with a flavoured gluten free pastry and come up with a melt-in-the-mouth pie which is tasty hot or cold.

1. Heat the oil in a saucepan and gently fry the garlic, carrot, celery and onion with 1 Tbsp coriander seeds and bay leaves for 10 mins until just softened but not browned.

2. Stir in the tomatoes and plenty of seasoning. Bring to the boil and simmer for 10 mins. Leave to cool, then discard the bay leaves, and stir in the beans and dill. Cover and chill until required.

3. To cook the pie, preheat the oven to 200°C, 180°C fan oven, 400°F, gas 6. Dust the work surface lightly with gluten free flour and roll out two thirds the pastry to fit a 24cm (9 ¾inch) round pie dish with rim. Transfer the pastry to the dish, and press together any cracks – the pastry is quite crumbly to work with. Trim to neaten the edge.

4. Spread the bean filling all over the pastry, and brush the edge with beaten egg. Roll out the remaining pastry as above and using a 6cm (2 ¼inch) crinkle edged round pastry cutter, stamp out at least 15 rounds, rerolling as necessary.

5. Carefully place round the edge of the pie dish, overlapping on top of the pie filling. Place one in the centre and make a hole in it.

6. Put the dish on a baking tray. Brush the pastry with beaten egg and sprinkle with remaining coriander seeds. Bake in the oven for about 40 mins until the pastry is cooked and golden and the filling hot. Serve straight from the dish while warm or allow to cool and chill before serving.

Ingredients

- 2 Tbsp olive oil
- 2 garlic cloves, peeled and crushed
- 1 carrot, peeled and finely chopped
- 1 stick celery, trimmed and finely chopped
- 1 small onion, peeled and finely chopped
- 5 tsp coriander (cilantro) seeds, lightly crushed
- 2 bay leaves
- 500g (1lb 2oz) creamed tomatoes or passata
- Salt and freshly ground black pepper
- 350g (12oz) cooked butterbeans
- 3 Tbsp freshly chopped dill
- 1 quantity of gluten free pastry, made with half fine cornmeal and half brown rice flour
- 1 egg, beaten, to glaze

Ratatouille Pie

Serves: 6 Preparation: 35 mins plus cooling Cooking: 1 hour 25 mins

Ingredients

4 Tbsp olive oil

2 ½ tsp coriander (cilantro)
seeds, lightly crushed

1 small onion, peeled and finely
chopped

2 garlic cloves, peeled and finely
chopped

1 each small red and yellow peppers,
deseeded and finely chopped

1 medium aubergine (eggplant),
trimmed and cut into cubes

350ml (12fl.oz) sieved tomatoes

1 medium courgette (zucchini),
trimmed and finely diced

1 bouquet garni — see below

Salt and freshly ground black
pepper

1 tsp caster (superfine) sugar

1 quantity oil pastry, made up with
olive oil and 2 Tbsp sun dried
tomato paste added, less 2
Tbsp water

One of my favourite vegetable dishes, ratatouille is a true taste of summer. Usually the vegetables are quite chunky but for a pie filling it is best to cut them up a bit smaller. There is no need to salt the aubergine for this recipe.

1. Heat 3 Tbsp oil in a large saucepan and gently fry 1½ tsp coriander seeds, onion, garlic and peppers for 10 mins until softened but not browned. Add the aubergine and cook, stirring, for 1 minute then pour over the sieved tomatoes and add the bouquet garni and seasoning. Bring to the boil, cover and simmer gently for 10 mins.

2. Stir in the courgette, replace the lid and to continue to cook for 10 mins until just tender, but not too soft. Stir in the sugar and leave to cool. Discard the bouquet garni and season to taste.

3. Make up the oil pastry. Preheat the oven to 200°C, 180°C fan oven, 400°F, gas 6. Roll out just over half the pastry on a lightly floured surface to fit a 23cm (9inch) diameter, 3.5cm (1½inch) deep pie plate or tin with rim. Trim to neaten the edge, and spread with the ratatouille filling. Brush the edge with water.

4. Roll out the remaining pastry as above to fit the top of the pie plate and lay on top. Press the edges together to seal and make a hole in the centre. Put the plate on a baking tray, brush with remaining oil and sprinkle with remaining coriander seeds. Bake for 45–50 mins until lightly golden and piping hot. Serve hot or cold.

Bouquet garni:

A selection of aromatic herbs used to flavour stocks, soups and casseroles. They are tied together in a bundle with string and are easily discarded before serving. Make your own from 2 – 3 sprigs of parsley, a sprig of thyme and rosemary, a bay leaf and celery leaf.

Filo Indian Samosas

Makes: 12   Preparation: 30 mins plus cooling   Cooking: 36 mins

Usually these tasty Indian snacks are made with a dough-like pastry, but filo makes a convenient casing which cooks to a crisp. Chop the vegetables quite small (or grate if you prefer) so that they cook quickly and fit neatly into the triangular samosa shape.

1. Put the spice seeds in a small frying pan and place over a medium heat and stir for 3–4 mins until lightly toasted. Cool slightly then lightly crush.

2. Meanwhile, melt the ghee or butter in a frying pan until bubbling and gently fry the garlic, ginger, onion, crushed seeds and finely chopped vegetables, and cook, stirring for about 20 mins until just tender. Leave to cool then stir in the onion seeds, coriander and plenty of seasoning.

3. Cut each sheet of filo into 3 long strips. Working on one strip at a time centre about 25g (1oz) of the vegetables at one end.

4. Fold the end of the pastry strip over to make a triangular turnover shape. Keep folding over until you reach the end of the strip, then brush the end with water and fold again to seal and form a multi-layered triangle. Continue filling and folding until you have made 12 samosas. Cover and chill until required.

5. To cook, heat the oil for deep frying to 190°C/375°F and fry the samosas in 3 batches for 3–4 mins, turning halfway through, until crisp and golden. Drain well and serve hot.

Variations

You can oven bake these samosas if preferred. You need to melt another 50g (2oz) ghee or butter and use to brush the pastry strips as you fold them up. Place on a baking tray lined with baking parchment, brush with remaining melted ghee or butter and bake in a preheated oven at 190°C, 170°C fan oven, 375°F, gas 5, for about 20 mins.

Ingredients

- 1 tsp each mustard seeds, cumin seeds and coriander (cilantro) seeds
- 25g (1oz) ghee or butter
- 1 garlic clove, peeled and crushed
- 2cm (3/4 inch) piece root ginger, peeled and grated
- 1 medium onion, peeled and finely chopped
- 175g (6oz) carrot, peeled and finely chopped
- 175g (6oz) potato, peeled and finely chopped
- 1 tsp black onion seeds
- 2 Tbsp freshly chopped coriander (cilantro)
- Salt and freshly ground black pepper
- 4 large sheets of filo pastry
- Vegetable oil for deep frying

Blue Cheese, Celery and Pear Crostata

Serves: 4   Preparation: 20 mins   Cooking: 30 mins

Ingredients

1 quantity double cheese pastry

2 small sweet, ripe pears, cored

2 sticks celery, trimmed and
        thinly sliced

115g (4oz) blue cheese, crumbled

25g (1oz) walnut pieces

1 egg, beaten, to glaze

Celery leaves to garnish

A crostata is an Italian pie which is formed simply on a baking tray and has a folded edge to hold in the filling. It's the perfect solution for using very short pastry or if you don't want to go to the extra bother of using a tin.

1. Preheat the oven to 200°C, 180°C fan oven, 400°F, gas 6. Line the work surface with a large sheet of baking parchment and dust lightly with flour. Roll out the pastry in a round to approx. 28cm (11inch) diameter. Carefully slide the pastry on the parchment on to a large baking tray. Cut down the parchment to fit the baking tray.

2. Slice the pears thinly and arrange all over the pastry to within 5cm (2inch) of the edge. Sprinkle with celery, blue cheese and walnut pieces.

3. Carefully fold in the pastry edge, pleating it as you go, to partially cover some of the filling. Press the pastry edge lightly to keep in place.

4. Brush the pastry with egg and bake for about 30 mins until the pastry is golden and crisp. Best served warm, garnished with celery leaves.

Variations

These pastries look rustic yet stunning and can be varied using different pastries and fillings. They work best with fillings that require little cooking and are firm in texture. Ring the changes by using sliced apple, fresh fig or even halved seedless grapes instead of pear.

Flaky Baby Tomato Pie

Serves: 2-3 Preparation: 20 mins Cooking: 20 mins

A colourful creation that will get your taste buds tingling. Simple to prepare, yet guaranteed to impress - everyone will think you've spent hours in the kitchen putting this one together! Yellow tomatoes look stunning when available, but all red works just as well.

1. Preheat the oven to 220°C, 200°C fan oven, 425°F, gas 7. Line a large baking tray with baking parchment. Roll out the pastry on a lightly floured surface to a rectangle 27 x 18cm (10½ x 7inch). Score the pastry 1cm (½inch) all round the edge, and then score the edge diagonally with a knife. Brush the edge with egg.

2. Mix the garlic and rosemary into the pesto and spread over the inner area of pastry. Arrange the tomatoes, side by side, alternate side up, on top in a single layer.

3. Drizzle with balsamic, sprinkle with sugar and season well. Sprinkle with a few rosemary sprigs and bake in the oven for about 20 mins until crisp and golden and the tomatoes are just tender. Discard the cooked rosemary.

4. To serve, carefully transfer the tart to a serving platter or board. Sprinkle over the crumbled cheese, garnish with extra fresh rosemary sprigs and serve immediately.

Variations
For a simplified version, spread the pastry case with regular green pesto. Top with the tomatoes and drizzle with olive oil before baking. Serve with shavings of fresh Parmesan cheese scattered over the top.

Ingredients

½ quantity flaky pastry,
1 egg, beaten, to glaze
2 garlic clove, peeled and crushed
1 Tbsp freshly chopped rosemary
   or 1 tsp dried
4 Tbsp red pesto sauce
275g (9 ½ oz) assorted baby
   plum tomatoes, halved
Dash of balsamic vinegar
1 tsp caster (superfine) sugar
Salt and freshly ground black
   pepper
A few small sprigs fresh
   rosemary
50g (2oz) firm goat's cheese,
   crumbled

Spanikopita

Makes: 9 Slices   Preparation: 40 mins plus cooling   Cooking: 1 hour 15 mins

Ingredients

4 Tbsp olive oil

1 medium onion, peeled and
    chopped

1 bunch spring onions (scallions),
    trimmed and white and green
    parts chopped

500g (1lb 2oz) spinach,
    trimmed and shredded

A small bunch fresh dill, chopped,
    or 4 tsp dried dill

A small bunch fresh continental
    (flat leaf) parsley, chopped

200g (7oz) feta cheese, finely
    crumbled

3 eggs, beaten

Freshly ground black pepper

75g (2½ oz) butter, melted

12 large sheets

In Greece, this pie is made during the Lenten fast, and contains no cheese, eggs or milk. This is the version many of us are more familiar with and it is best eaten on the same day as baking.

1. Heat the oil in a large saucepan and cook the onion and spring onions for 5 mins, stirring occasionally, until softened, but not browned. Add half the spinach, mix well, cover with a lid, reduce the heat and cook gently for 5 mins, stirring occasionally, until wilted down. Transfer to a heatproof plate.

2. Pack the remaining spinach in the same saucepan and add 2 Tbsp water. Cover and cook for 5 mins, stirring occasionally, until wilted down. Mix in the oniony spinach mixture to the saucepan, and cook, stirring, for a further 5 mins, then drain well through a sieve or colander, pressing the vegetables against the sides to extract as much water as possible. Leave to cool, then blot with kitchen paper and put in a bowl. Stir in the feta cheese, beaten eggs and plenty of black pepper and mix well.

3. Preheat the oven to 170°C, 150°C fan oven, 325°F, Gas 3. Grease and line a 25 x 17.5 x 3 cm (10 x 6 ¾ x 1¼ inch) cake tin with baking parchment, then brush with butter.

4. Brush a sheet of filo with butter and use to line the tin, folding it and carefully pressing it into the sides and corners of the tin so that the pastry fits snugly with a little overhanging the edges. Brush all over with butter and lay another sheet on top, folding it and pressing it down as before. Continue the buttering, layering and pressing process until you have used 6 sheets.

5 . Spread the spinach mixture into the pastry case, packing it evenly into the corners. Brush a sheet of filo with butter and fold to fit the top of the tin. Lay directly on the spinach and fold over the overlapping edges.

6 . Repeat this process, using up the remaining sheet. Brush the top with any remaining butter and bake in the centre of the oven for about 1 hour until the pastry is crisp and golden brown all over. Cut into 9 wedges and serve hot or slightly warm.

Mini Beany Empanadas

Makes: 9   Preparation: 35 mins plus cooling   Cooking: 13 mins

These Mexican-style snacks are more typically made with tortilla dough as a casing, but rough puff pastry makes a good alternative and gives a wonderfully soft flaky case; perfect for bite-sized party snacks.

1. Heat the oil in a frying pan and gently fry the garlic, chilli to taste, and spring onions for 2–3 mins until just softened. Set aside to cool.

2. Put the beans in a bowl and mix in the sweetcorn, coriander and chilli onion mixture. Season well.

3. Roll out the pastry on a lightly floured surface to form a 27cm (11inch) square. Using a 9cm (3 ¾inch) round cutter, stamp out 9 rounds of pastry. Divide the filling between the centre of each. Brush the edge with water and bring up the edges, pressing them together to seal well. Place on a board lined with baking parchment, cover and chill until required.

4. Heat about 2cm (¾inch) oil in a large deep frying pan until hot. Cook the empanadas over a medium heat for 4–5 mins on each side, until golden. Drain well and serve warm. Delicious accompanied with a chopped salad of avocado, tomato and fresh coriander with a squeeze of lime.

Variations

If preferred, you can bake these pastries. Place on a large baking tray lined with baking parchment and bake in a preheated oven at 220°C, 200°C fan oven, 425°F, gas 7, for about 15 mins until crisp and golden.

Ingredients

2 tsp olive oil
2 garlic cloves
½ –1 tsp dried chilli flakes
4 spring onions (scallions), trimmed and chopped
115g (4oz) cooked kidney beans, mashed
115g (4oz) cooked sweetcorn
2 Tbsp freshly chopped coriander (cilantro)
Salt and freshly ground black pepper
½ quantity rough puff pastry
Vegetable oil for shallow frying

Afternoon Tea Egg and Cress Handfuls

Makes: 8   Preparation: 20 mins plus cooling   Cooking: 20 mins

Ingredients

½ quantity flaky pastry,
1 egg, beaten
4 hard boiled eggs, peeled
4 Tbsp mayonnaise
½ tsp English mustard, optional
Salt and freshly ground black
    pepper
1 box/carton baby watercress or
    mustard and cress, rinsed and
    trimmed

I've made several versions of these pastries and settled on this one as my favourite. You can make up the cases 2 or 3 days in advance of serving, and of course, use them with any savoury or sweet filling you may prefer.

1. Preheat the oven to 220°C, 200°C fan oven, 425°F, gas 7. Lightly grease 8 x 7cm (2 ¾ inch) diameter, 3½ cm (1 ¼ inch) deep muffin tins. Roll the pastry thinly on a lightly floured surface to make a rectangle 40 x 20cm (16 x 8inch). Cut into 8 squares.

2. Press each square gently into a muffin tin and line each with a small square of baking parchment. Half fill with baking beans or raw pulses or rice.

3. Bake in the oven for 10 mins to set the pastry. Carefully remove the beans or rice and the paper. Prick the bases, brush with egg and cook for a further 8–10 mins until golden and cooked through. Transfer to a wire rack to cool.

4. For the filling, mash the hardboiled eggs and mix with the mayonnaise, mustard if using and seasoning to taste. Stir in half the watercress or mustard and cress.

5. To serve, spoon the egg mixture into each pastry case. Sprinkle with the remaining cress and dust with black pepper to serve.

Variations

For a more contemporary twist, replace the cress with small leaves of wild rocket.

Creamy Roast Garlic Mushroom Pie

Serves: 3-4   Preparation: 25 mins plus cooling   Cooking: 45 mins

Meaty, nutty flavoured mushrooms like Portabella make the best pie fillings as they are both fleshy and tasty. They are robust enough to stand up to reheating. If unavailable, use field or flat mushrooms, but peel first.

1. Preheat the oven to 200°C, 180°C fan oven, 400°F, gas 6. Drizzle a shallow sided roasting tray with 1 Tbsp oil and arrange the mushrooms on top. Mix the remaining oil with the garlic and spoon over the mushrooms. Season generously. Sprinkle with a few thyme sprigs and bake in the oven for 15 mins until tender. Leave to cool. Discard the thyme.

2. Drain the mushrooms, reserving any pan juices, and slice thickly. Put the mushrooms and cheese in a 18 x 14 x 5cm (6 x 5 ¾ x 2 inch) pie dish with a wide rim. Mix the reserved baking juices with the white wine and cream and pour over the mushrooms. Season to taste.

3. To make up the pie, roll out the pastry quite thickly on a lightly floured surface to just larger than the pie dish. Carefully cut some of the excess pastry into thin strips, flatten slightly and secure on to the edge of the pie dish with water. Brush with egg.

4. Transfer the rolled out pastry to the top and press down on to the edge to seal. Make a hole in the centre and brush all over with egg. Sprinkle with a few more sprigs of thyme.

5. Put the dish on a baking tray and bake for about 30 mins until risen and golden. Serve immediately with sprinkled with fresh thyme if liked.

Variations
For a richer pie, cover with ½ quantity flaky or rough puff pastry.

Ingredients

3 Tbsp olive oil

500g (1lb 2oz) Portabella (large) mushrooms, wiped

2 garlic cloves, peeled and finely chopped

Salt and freshly ground black pepper

A small bunch fresh thyme

200g (7oz) Gorgonzola cheese, cubed

50ml (2fl.oz) dry white wine

50ml (2fl.oz) double cream

¾ quantity suet crust pastry, made with vegetable suet, and 1 Tbsp freshly chopped thyme or 1 tsp dried thyme added

1 egg, beaten, to glaze

Free Form Bean and Pea Pies

Serves: 6   Preparation: 25 mins plus cooling   Cooking: 24 mins

Ingredients

150g (5oz) shelled peas

150g (5oz) shelled broad (fava) beans

1 quantity soft cheese pastry

1 ½ tsp ground cumin

6 spring onions (scallions), trimmed and white and green parts finely chopped

2 eggs beaten

150ml (¼ pt) double cream

Salt and freshly ground black pepper

I first discovered a variation of this pastry when I was researching recipes for a Cuban cook book. Cream cheese makes a short and slightly flaky pastry which is an absolute joy to eat with fresh sweet spring vegetables.

1. Preheat the oven to 220°C, 200°C fan oven, 425°F, gas 7. Line a large baking tray with baking parchment. Bring a saucepan of water to the boil and blanch the peas and beans for 4 mins. Drain well and rinse in cold water. Set aside in cold water.

2. Divide the pastry in to 6. On a lightly floured surface, gently roll out into 6 roughly shaped 20cm (8in) circles. Drain the peas and beans well and pat dry with absorbent kitchen paper. Put in a bowl and mix in the cumin and all but 2 Tbsp spring onions.

3. Carefully pile on to the centre of each pastry circle, and brush the edges with a little of the egg. Bring up the sides of the pastry, pleating and pinching together to enclose the vegetables and make a case, but leaving the top open – make sure you seal the sides well to avoid the filling leaking during cooking..

4. Beat 2 eggs together with the cream and plenty of seasoning, and pour in to each pie. Bake for about 20 mins until golden. Sprinkle with remaining spring onions and serve hot or cold with wholegrain mustard.

Variation:

You can follow the same basic recipe used above but substitute the peas and beans with blueberries and raspberries to make dessert pies. Mix 2 or 3 Tbsp caster sugar and 1 tsp vanilla extract into the egg and cream mixture and then bake as above.

White Nut and Pesto Filo Pies

Serves: 8   Preparation: 40 mins plus cooling   Cooking: 28 mins

These creations are perfect for an alternative Christmas dinner and homemade pesto really makes a difference to the flavour of the baked pies.

Ingredients

150g (5oz) butter or margarine

1 onion, peeled and finely chopped

250g (9oz) assorted unsalted
   almonds, pine nuts and
   cashews, chopped

75g (2½ oz) fresh white
   breadcrumbs

Salt and freshly ground black
   pepper

Pinch of ground mace or nutmeg

1 egg, beaten

8 large sheets filo pastry

1 quantity fresh pesto sauce —
   see below

1. Melt 50g (2oz) butter or margarine in a frying pan and gently fry the onion for 7–8 mins until softened but not browned. Cool for 20 mins.

2. Put the nuts in a bowl and stir in the breadcrumbs along with plenty of seasoning, spice and the onion mixture. Add the egg and mix well to form a stiff stuffing mixture. Set aside.

3. Preheat the oven to 200°C, 180°C fan oven, 400°F, gas 6. Line 2 large baking trays with baking parchment. Melt the remaining butter or margarine. Working on one sheet of pastry at a time, brush with melted fat, fold in half and brush again.

4. Spoon one eighth of the nut filling on one side of the pastry to within 2cm (¾inch) of the edges; flatten slightly and spoon one eighth of the pesto on top. Fold over the edges over the nut filling and brush the edges with butter.

5. Keep folding the pastry over until you have an enveloped shape parcel. Press the edges together to seal and transfer to a baking tray.

6. Continue the pie making to use up all the pastry and filling. Brush with remaining butter, make a slit in the top of each and bake in the oven for about 20 mins until golden and crisp. Best served warm.

Homemade pesto (makes 200g-7oz)
Put 1 peeled garlic clove in a blender or food processor with 15g (½oz) fresh basil, 75g (2½oz) pine nuts, 50g (2oz) finely grated fresh Parmesan cheese and 4 Tbsp extra virgin olive oil. Season well and blend until smooth. Store in a sealed jar in the refrigerator for up to 10 days.

Golden Vegetable Pasties

Serves: 8   Preparation: 30 mins plus cooling   Cooking: 33 mins

Mustard goes very well with sweet vegetables and the natural sweetness is enhanced by grated apple. For extra zing, mix in some finely grated orange zest.

1. Put the carrots and ginger in a saucepan; cover with water and bring to the boil. Cook for 7–8 mins. Drain well, return to the saucepan and mash with a fork. Leave to cool.

2. Meanwhile, bring a small saucepan of water to the boil and cook the baby corn for 4–5 mins until tender. Drain well, leave to cool then mix into the carrot.

3. Peel, core and grate the apple. Mix into the cooked vegetables along with the mustard and plenty of seasoning.

4. Preheat the oven to 220°C, 200°C fan oven, 425°F, gas 7. Line a large baking tray with baking parchment. Divide the pastry in 2 and roll out each half on a lightly floured surface to form a 30cm (12inch) square. Using a 15cm (6inch) saucer or round cutter, stamp out 4 rounds of pastry from each.

5. Divide the filling between the centre of each pastry round. Brush the edge with water and fold in half; press the edges together and carefully crimp the edges between your thumb and forefinger.

6. Transfer to the baking tray; brush with the egg and sprinkle lightly with mustard seeds. Bake in the oven for about 20 mins until golden and puffy. Best served warm.

Variations

Try parsnip, turnip or swede instead of carrot; you can also use the flesh of butternut squash. Adjust the initial boiling period accordingly to make sure the root vegetable cooks properly.

Ingredients

- 300g (10oz) carrots, peeled and chopped
- 2.5cm (1inch) root ginger, peeled and finely chopped
- 150g (5oz) baby corn, trimmed and sliced
- 1 eating apple
- 2 Tbsp wholegrain mustard
- Salt and freshly ground black pepper
- 1 quantity wholewheat rough puff pastry,
- 1 egg, beaten
- 1 Tbsp mustard seeds, lightly crushed

East meets West

Serves: 4   Preparation: 30 mins plus cooling   Cooking: 34 mins

Some vegetables are too delicate for conventional pie cooking. For this recipe, the pastry part gets cooked first, and then is filled with "just cooked" Asian vegetables and topped with a crisp crumb to finish.

1. Preheat the oven to 200°C, 180°C fan oven, 400°F, gas 6. Roll out the pastry on a lightly floured surface to fit a 18cm (9inch) diameter, 4cm (1 ¾inch) deep pie tin with a rim. Trim to neaten the edge, then press the edge with a with a fork.

2. Place a circle of baking parchment in the centre. Fill with baking beans or raw pulses or rice. Stand the tin on a baking tray and bake for 10 mins. Carefully remove the beans or rice and paper. Prick the base all over with a fork and return to the oven for a further 8–10 mins until the pastry is lightly golden and cooked through. Set aside, in the tin, on a wire rack. If preferred, when cold, slip the pastry case out of the tin.

3. Meanwhile, heat 2 Tbsp oil in a frying pan until bubbling and stir fry the breadcrumbs for 5 mins until crisp and lightly golden. Remove from the heat and stir in the sesame seeds and chives, and keep warm.

4. Heat the remaining oil in a wok or large frying pan and stir fry the garlic, chilli, spring onion, broccoli and baby corn for 2–3 mins. Add the pak choi and continue to stir fry for a further 2–3 mins. Add the sauce, and stir fry for a further 2–3 mins until just tender.

5. Spoon the vegetables into the pastry case using a slotted spoon. Sprinkle the crumbs on top and serve immediately.

Tip: Once assembled, you can keep this pie on a low heat (about 150°C, 130°C fan oven, 300°F, gas 2) for up to 20 mins until you are ready to serve.

Ingredients

- ½ quantity shortcrust pastry, with 3 Tbsp toasted sesame seeds added
- 3 Tbsp vegetable oil
- 50g (2oz) fresh white breadcrumbs
- 2 Tbsp toasted sesame seeds
- 2 Tbsp freshly chopped chives
- 2 garlic cloves, peeled and chopped
- 1 red chilli, deseeded and thinly sliced
- 4 spring onions (scallions), trimmed and chopped
- 100g (3 ½ oz) very small sprouting broccoli, trimmed
- 100g (3 ½ oz) baby corn, trimmed and sliced lengthways
- 100g (3 ½ oz) baby pak choi leaves, trimmed
- 3 Tbsp oyster sauce or 1 Tbsp dark soy sauce plus 2 Tbsp sweet chilli sauce

Sweet

French-style Custard Pies

Serves: 8   Preparation: 40 mins plus cooling   Cooking: 30 mins

Ingredients

3 large egg yolks

115g (4oz) caster (superfine)
   sugar

3 Tbsp plain
   (all purpose) flour

300ml (½ pt) whole milk

1 tsp good quality vanilla extract

1 quantity pâté sucrée

1 egg, beaten, for glazing

1 Tbsp icing (confectioner's)
   sugar

Certainly too good for circus clowns, I discovered this rich dessert looking through a French cookery book. It comes from the Basque region, and is a thick custard tart referred to as a cake. These mini versions are rich and decadent. Perfect served with fresh soft fruit or poached pears.

1. Grease 8 x 7cm (2 ¾inch) diameter 3½cm (1½inch) deep muffin tins. First, make the filling. Whisk the egg yolks together with the sugar until thick and pale. Sieve over the flour and fold in using a metal spoon. Gradually whisk in the vanilla and milk. Pour into a saucepan and cook over a low heat, stirring, until quite thick, taking care not to burn. Cover the surface with a sheet of buttered greaseproof paper and leave to cool.

2. Meanwhile, roll out three quarters of the pastry on a lightly floured surface and stamp out 8 x 10cm (4inch) circles to fit into the prepared tins. Gently press the pastry into each tin. Neaten the edges and chill until required.

3. Spoon cold custard in to the pastry cases to almost fill. Roll out the remaining pastry thinly and cut out 8 x 6cm (2½inch) rounds. Brush the inside edge of the pastry cases with beaten egg and gently press a pastry circle on top of each. Pinch the edges together to seal. Make a small hole in the centre of each. Cover and chill for 30 mins.

4. Preheat the oven to 190°C, 170°C fan oven, 375°F, gas 5. Brush the top of the pastry with egg and bake in the oven for about 25 mins until golden and firm to the touch. Allow to cool for 10 mins in the tins, then carefully run a knife round the edge of each to remove them from the tin. Transfer to a wire rack to cool. Dust with icing sugar and serve cold with fruit and pouring cream.

Vanilla Prune Puff

Serves: 6   Preparation: 20 mins plus cooling   Cooking: 20 mins

Not many ingredients necessary to make this fruity, sweet French-style pastry. Choose the softest, juiciest best quality prunes you can find for this recipe; Agen prunes are particularly good if you can track them down.

Ingredients

½ quantity puff pastry
25g (1oz) unsalted butter, softened
1 vanilla pod
2 Tbsp caster (superfine) sugar
1 Tbsp vanilla sugar
300g (10oz) soft pitted prunes
1 egg, beaten, to glaze
1 Tbsp icing (confectioner's) sugar

1. Preheat the oven to 220°C, 200°C fan oven, 425°F, gas 7. Line a baking tray with baking parchment. Divide the pastry in two. On a lightly floured surface, roll out one half to make a circular shape about 23cm (9inch) in diameter. Carefully transfer to the lined baking tray.

2. Put the butter in a small bowl. Split the vanilla pod in half and scrape out the black seedy paste from both halves, and mix into the butter. Spread the vanilla butter sparingly all over the pastry round to within 1cm (½inch) of the edge, and sprinkle with the sugars.

3. Arrange the prunes neatly and evenly on top. Brush the edge of the pastry with water.

4. Roll out the other half of the pastry in the same way, and place on top of the prunes. Press the pastry layers together to seal, and "knock up" the edges to neaten and create a good seal.

5. Brush the top of the pastry with egg and prick lightly with a fork. Bake in the oven for about 20 mins until richly golden brown and puffed up. Best served warm, dusted with icing sugar and accompanied with crème fraîche.

Deep Dish Sweet Spiced Apple Pie

Serves: 8   Preparation: 40 mins plus cooling   Cooking: 70 mins

Ingredients

1 ½ quantity sweet shortcrust
       pie pastry
900g (2lb) cooking apples
Finely grated rind and juice of 1
       large lemon
115g (4oz) light brown sugar
2 Tbsp cornflour (cornstarch)
1 ½ tsp ground cinnamon
50g (2oz) sultanas
25g (1oz) unsalted butter
1 egg, beaten
1 Tbsp caster (superfine) sugar

A classic family dessert pie, poopular with all generations. There's lots of apple in the filling in this recipe, and it's delicately flavoured with spices and lemon.

1. Preheat the oven to 200°C, 180°C fan oven, 400°F, gas 6. Roll out two thirds of the pastry on a lightly floured surface and use to line a 23cm (9 inch) diameter, 4cm (1½inch) deep pie dish with a rim. Trim and keep the trimmings.

2. Meanwhile, peel, core and thinly slice the apples. Place in a bowl and toss in the lemon rind and juice. In another bowl, mix the brown sugar, cornflour and spice together.

3. Sprinkle a little of the sugar mixture over the base of the pastry case, and mix the remainder into the apples along with the sultanas. Pile half of the apple mixture into the pastry case and push in a pie bird or funnel. Pile in the remaining apple (to come above the rim of the dish) and dot the top with the butter.

4. Roll out the remaining pastry as above to fit the top of the pie, and make a cross in the centre. Brush the pie edge with egg and press the pie lid on top. Trim and seal the edge. Roll out the trimmings and cut out apple and leaf shapes and secure on the pie with egg.

6. Brush the pastry top with egg and sprinkle with caster sugar . Stand the dish on a baking tray and bake for 30 mins to evenly brown then reduce the oven temperature to 180°C, 160°C fan oven, 350°F, gas 4. Cover the pie with foil and continue to bake for a further 40 mins until the apple is tender – push a skewer into the centre to see if cooked. Serve the pie straight from the dish, hot or cold, with custard or ice cream.

Berry Fruitfuls

Serves: 4   Preparation: 50 mins plus chilling and cooling   Cooking: 35 mins

1. Preheat the oven to 200°C, 180°C fan oven, 400°F, gas 6. Sieve the flour and salt into a bowl and rub in the butter until well blended. Stir in 75g (2½oz) caster sugar and bind together with approx. 3 Tbsp cold water to bring the mixture together. Knead lightly to form a smooth dough. Wrap and chill for 30 mins.

2. Set aside one quarter of the pastry, then divide the remaining pastry into 4 pieces. On a lightly floured surface, roll each piece to fit a 4 x12cm (5inch) diameter, 3.5cm (1¼inch) deep rimless pie tin. Trim, cover and chill until required.

3. For the filling, put 200g (7oz) berries in a saucepan with 1 Tbsp water. Bring to the boil, cover and simmer for 3 – 4 mins until very soft. Cool slightly then push through a nylon sieve to make a purée. Return to the saucepan.

4. Mix the cornflour with 2 Tbsp water to form a paste and add to the fruit purée along with all but 2 Tbsp of the remaining caster sugar . Bring to the boil, stirring, and cook until thickened. Remove from the heat and stir in the reserved berries. Leave to cool.

5. Spoon the cooled filling into the pastry cases. Roll out the remaining pastry thinly and cut out 4 x 10cm (4inch) round lids. Brush the inside edge of the pastry case with egg white and push the the lids on top, press the edges together to seal well. Place on a large baking tray. Make small holes in the centre of each.

6. Roll out the trimmings to make fruit decorations. Brush the pie top with egg white, stick on the decorations if using and dredge with remaining caster sugar . Bake for 30 mins or until golden. Serve hot or cold with pouring cream.

Ingredients

250g (9oz) plain
    (all purpose) flour
¼ tsp salt
150g (5oz) unsalted butter
175g (6oz) caster (superfine)
    sugar
1 egg white, lightly beaten
600g (1lb 5oz) prepared
    blueberries, blackberries and
    raspberries
1 Tbsp cornflour (cornstarch)

Coconut and Lime Meringue Pie

Serves: 6   Preparation: 30 mins plus cooling   Cooking: 35 mins

Ingredients

½ quantity sweet shortcrust
  pastry
2 Tbsp cornflour (cornstarch)
175g (6oz) caster (superfine)
  sugar
Juice and finely grated rind of
  3 limes
300ml (½ pt) canned coconut
  milk
A few drops green food colouring,
  optional
2 medium egg whites

Rich and exotic flavours of coconut and lime give
a delicious, contemporary twist to a classic lemon
meringue pie.

1. Preheat the oven to 200°C, 180°C fan oven, 400°F, gas 6. On a lightly floured surface, roll out the pastry thinly to fit a 23cm (9inch) diameter, 3cm (1½inch) deep) pie or flan tin with rim. Fit the pastry to the tin, trim and place a circle of baking parchment in the centre. Fill with baking beans or raw pulses or rice.

2. Put the tin on a baking tray and bake for 10 mins. Carefully remove the beans or rice and paper. Prick the base all over with a fork and return to the oven for a further 8–10 mins until the pastry is lightly golden and cooked through. Set aside, in the tin, on a wire rack. Remove the pastry case from the tin.

3. Meanwhile, mix the cornflour , 75g (2½oz) caster sugar and lime juice together in a saucepan to form a paste. Add the coconut milk and cook over a medium heat, stirring all the time, until just boiling then simmer for 1 minute. Stir in the lime zest and add a few drops green colouring if using. Pour into the pastry case and set aside to cool completely.

4. In a clean bowl, whisk the egg whites until very stiff and gradually whisk in the remaining sugar to make a thick, glossy meringue.

5. Pipe or spoon the meringue over the lime filling to cover completely. Put the pie on a baking tray and bake in the oven for about 10 mins until evenly browned. Serve hot or cold.

Variation

If you prefer something more traditional, replace the lime rind and juice with the juice and rind of one large lemon, and use double cream instead of coconut milk.

Quince "Pasties"

Ingredients

1 quantity soft cheese pastry

250g (9oz) membrillo (quince
      paste), cut into 16 portions

1 egg white, lightly beaten

2 Tbsp caster (superfine) sugar
      mixed with 1 tsp ground
      cinnamon

A melt-in-the-mouth variation of the simple jam (jelly) turnover. Use your favourite jam, pie filling or thinly sliced fruit if you prefer. For complete decadence, use chocolate or caramel spread. Allow the pastries to cool for a few mins before serving as the filling retains heat and may scald.

1. Line 2 baking trays with baking parchment. Lightly dust the work surface with flour. Divide the dough into 16 equal pieces. Taking one piece of dough at a time, roll it into a ball and then roll out with a rolling pin to form a 10 cm (4 inch) circle.

2. Place a portion of quince paste in the centre, and brush the edge lightly with water. Carefully fold the pastry over, and secure the edges by pinching together. Sit fold side down on the work surface to flatten the bottom and then place on the baking tray. Repeat to make 16. Cover loosely and chill for 30 mins.

3. Preheat the oven to 200°C, 180°C fan oven, 400°F, gas 6. Discard the covering, brush lightly with beaten egg white and sprinkle lightly with cinnamon sugar. Bake for about 15 mins until golden and crisp. Cool for 15 mins then serve while still warm. Delicious served with clotted cream.

Variation

You can use this idea for make alternative mince pies for serving at Christmas by replacing the jam (jelly) with readymade mince meat. Follow the above method using regular sweet shortcrust or puff pastry if preferred.

Cherry Nice Chocolate Pie

Serves: 8   Preparation: 35 mins plus cooling and standing   Cooking: 40 mins

1. Make and bake pastry case as directed below using two thirds of the pastry. Reduce the oven temperature to 180°C, 160°C fan oven, 350°F, gas 4. Spread the jam (jelly) over the base of the pastry case and arrange the cherry halves on top. Set aside.

2. Put the butter and chocolate in a heatproof bowl over a saucepan of gently simmering water until melted. Remove from the water and set aside. Whisk the eggs and sugar together until pale and creamy.

3. Gently fold the melted chocolate and butter into the egg mixture and spoon over the pastry. Smooth the surface.

4. Roll out the remaining chocolate pastry to a roughly shaped rectangle approx 25cm (10inch) long. Cut into approx. 12 thin strips, rerolling as necessary and arrange on top of the pie to form a lattice. Secure the edges on to the edge of the pastry case using a little water.

5. Put the tin on a baking tray and bake for about 25 mins until the top has formed a crust, and the pastry is set. Stand for 10 mins before removing from the tin to serve hot, or allow to cool in the tin and chill for at least 1 hour. Delicious with vanilla or chocolate ice cream.

Chocolate pie pastry (makes 375g (13oz))

Sieve plain flour, cocoa, salt and caster (superfine) sugar into a bowl. Rub in unsalted butter to form a mixture that resembles fresh breadcrumbs. Mix in egg yolk and a few drops of vanilla extract and bring the mixture together adding 3-4 tsp whole milk if necessary. Knead gently to form a firm dough. Wrap and chill for 30 mins. Roll out two thirds of the pastry thinly on a lightly floured surface to fit a 24cm (9½ inch) diameter, 4cm (1¾inch) deep pie tin with rim. Prick the base all over with a fork and bake in the oven at 200°C, 180 C fan oven, 400 F, gas 6 for about 15 mins until set and firm to the touch. The remaining pastry can be used as a pastry lattice for the top.

Ingredients

1 quantity chocolate pie pastry – see below

6 Tbsp good quality cherry jam (jelly)

200g (7oz) fresh cherries, pitted and halved, or tinned

85g (3oz) unsalted butter

100g (3 ½ oz) dark 72% cocoa chocolate, broken into pieces

2 eggs, beaten

50g (2oz) caster (superfine) sugar

Cocoa powder and icing (confectioner's) sugar to dust

Chocolate Pie Pastry

175g (6oz) plain (all purpose) flour

1 ½ Tbsp cocoa

A pinch of salt

75g (3oz) caster (superfine) sugar

75g (3oz) unsalted butter

1 egg yolk

vanilla extract

whole milk if desired

Mini Lemon Roly Pollies

Makes: 4 Preparation: 20 mins Cooking: 25 mins

Ingredients

200g (7oz) self raising flour
Pinch of salt
100g (3½ oz) vegetable suet
75g (2½ oz) caster sugar
Finely grated rind 1 unwaxed
    lemon
150ml (¼ pt) freshly squeezed
    lemon juice
5 Tbsp good quality lemon curd
1 egg, beaten, for glazing
4 tsp Demerara sugar
Custard to serve

Roly Pollies are a traditional British nursery pudding usually made with jam. Here I combine the flavours from a sweet suet crust pudding from my childhood called Sussex Pond Pudding. This version is a bit kinder on the hips, but still extremely lemony and comforting.

1. Preheat the oven to 200°C, 180°C fan oven, 400°F, gas 6. Line a large baking tray with baking parchment. Make up the lemon suet crust by mixing together the flour, suet, sugar and lemon rind. Add enough of the lemon juice, mixing at the same time, to make a light, elastic dough.

2. Turn dough onto a lightly floured surface and knead very gently until smooth. Divide the mixture into 4 equal pieces. Roll out each piece to make a 12 x 16cm (5 x 6½inch) rectangle. Spread with the lemon curd to within 1cm (½inch) of the edges.

3. Brush the edges with beaten egg, and carefully roll up each one, starting from one of the shorter sides. Press lightly to seal the edge and place seam-side down on the baking tray.

4. Brush all over with beaten egg, sprinkle with Demerara sugar and bake for about 25 minutes until golden brown and risen – they will probably split on baking. Best served hot or warm with lots of custard.

Just Peachy Filo Crisp

Serves: 4   Preparation: 25 mins plus cooling   Cooking: 33 mins

Ingredients

1 unwaxed lemon

1 Tbsp cornflour (cornstarch)

4 Tbsp caster (superfine) sugar

6 cardamom pods, split

4 ripe peaches, peeled if preferred
  — see below

4 large sheets filo pastry

1 egg, beaten

2 tsp icing (confectioner's)
  sugar

This pie is perfect for summer when the juiciest, sweetest peaches are around. Cardamom spice has a citrusy note and therefore combines perfectly with fresh lemon.

1. Using a vegetable peeler, pare off 3 strips of lemon rind into a small saucepan. Add the juice and blend in the cornflour and 3 Tbsp sugar. Remove the black seeds from the cardamom pods and grind finely and add to the saucepan.

2. Gradually blend in 200ml (7fl.oz) cold water. Bring to the boil, stirring, and simmer gently for 1 minute. Remove from the heat; cover the top of the sauce directly with a piece of greaseproof paper and leave to cool.

3. Preheat the oven temperature to 200°C, 180°C fan oven, 400°F, gas 6. Halve and slice the peaches and place in a 900ml (1½pt) oval pie dish – or a dish approx. 20 x 15 x 4.5cm (8 x 6 x 1 ¾inch). Hold a sieve over the dish and strain the cold lemon sauce through on to the peaches.

4. Lay the sheets of pastry on the work surface and brush with egg, then scrunch up each sheet to make a loose "rosette" shape and arrange on top to cover the peaches – pull the pastry rosettes apart again if necessary.

5. Brush with more egg and sprinkle with remaining sugar. Put the dish on a baking tray and bake in the oven for about 30 mins until golden, crisp and hot. Serve immediately dusted with icing sugar.

How to peel peaches

Prick the stalk end of a ripe peach with a fork. Place in a heatproof bowl and cover with boiling water. Leave for about 30 seconds to loosen the skin, then plunge in to cold, iced water. Carefully peel away the skin. Brush with lemon juice to prevent discolouration.

Butterscotch Cream Pie

Serves: 6-8   Preparation: 30 mins plus cooling and chilling   Cooking: 20 mins

When I was at school, every now and then we would be given a dessert called butterscotch tart. I loved it. The pastry bit wasn't great but the butterscotch custard filling was gorgeous. This is my grown up version, and I use posh sweet pastry to suit my adult palate.

1. Preheat the oven to 190°C, 170°C fan oven, 375°F, gas 5. Roll out the pastry to fit a 23cm (9inch) diameter, 3.5cm (1½inch) deep pie tin or dish with rim. Trim to neaten the edge, prick the base all over with a fork and bake in the oven for about 15 mins until lightly golden and crisp. Leave to cool.

2. For the filling, melt the butter in a saucepan and mix in the sugar. Stir over a low heat until dissolved. Remove from the heat. Blend the cornflour with a little of the milk to make a paste, and mix the remaining milk into the buttery sugar.

3. Stir in the cornflour paste and return to the heat. Cook, stirring, bring to the boil and simmer for 1 minute, to make a thick custard sauce. Stir in the vanilla and salt.

4. Pour the hot custard into the pastry case and leave to cool, then chill for 1 hour.

5. To serve, spoon dollops of crème fraîche round the edge and sprinkle with crushed butterscotch. Delicious accompanied with fresh strawberries.

Ingredients

½ quantity pâté sucrée made up with a few drops vanilla extract added

150g (5oz) unsalted butter

150g (5oz) Demerara sugar

350ml (12fl.oz) whole milk

1 Tbsp cornflour (cornstarch)

3 Tbsp dark cho

1 tsp good quality vanilla extract

Pinch of salt

200g (7oz) crème fraîche

50g (2oz) butterscotch, crushed

Festive Fruit And Marzipan Pies

Serves: 12   Preparation: 30 mins plus cooling   Cooking: 30 mins

Once you've tried these, you'll never want to make a standard mince pie again. Using a hot water crust pastry case for mincemeat and marzipan means that these little pies aren't as sweet as the more traditional shortcrust pastry versions. I prefer to make the hot watercrust pastry for sweet pies using white vegetable fat instead of lard.

1. Preheat the oven to 200°C, 180°C fan oven, 400°F, gas 6. Make up the hot water crust pastry. Roll out the pastry thinly on a lightly floured surface and cut out 12 x 9cm (3½inch) rounds using a round pastry cutter, re-rolling as necessary. Gently press each circle into 7cm (2 ¾ inch) diameter, 3½ cm (1 ¼ inch) deep muffin tins. Discard the trimmings.

2. In a bowl, mix together the mincemeat, grated apple, cranberries and spice together. Spoon a portion of the fruity filling into each and pack down well. Stand the tins on a baking tray. Bake in the oven for about 30 mins until rich golden brown.

3. Meanwhile, roll out the marzipan thickly, and cut out 12 x 5cm (2inch) star shapes, re-rolling as necessary. Set aside.

4. When the pies are cooked, place a star on each pie. Loosen the edges of the pies with a round bladed knife and cool for 10 mins, before carefully removing from the tins and transferring to a wire rack. Best served warm, dusted with icing sugar and accompanied with pouring cream.

Ingredients

- ½ quantity hot watercrust pastry, made with white vegetable fat and plain (all purpose) flour
- 300g (10oz) mincemeat
- 150g (5oz) cooking apple, peeled, cored and grated
- 75g (2½ oz) dried cranberries
- 1 tsp ground mixed spice
- 100g (3½ oz) golden or natural marzipan
- 1 Tbsp icing (confectioner's) sugar

Plum and Almond Crostata

Serves: 6-8 Preparation: 30 mins plus cooling Cooking: 40 mins

Ingredients

1 quantity extra rich shortcrust
  pastry
200g (7oz) ground almonds
125g (4 ½ oz) caster
  (superfine) sugar
1 tsp good quality almond extract
2 eggs, beaten
350g (12oz) plums, washed,
  pitted and thickly sliced
25g (1oz) unsalted butter
2 Tbsp Demerara sugar

If you can find some greengages, try using them in this recipe. The almondy filling combines superbly with their fresh, fruity flavour. Otherwise, any other plum or even apricots work just as well in this free-form rustic pastry.

1. Preheat the oven to 200°C, 180°C fan oven, 400°F, gas 6. Line the work surface with a large sheet of baking parchment and dust lightly with flour. Roll out the pastry in a round to approx. 36cm (14½inch) diameter. Trim the edge to neaten, then carefully slide the pastry on the paper on to a large baking tray. Cut down the parchment to fit the baking tray.

2. Mix together the ground almonds, caster sugar and almond extract. Bind together well using one of the eggs. Press the almond paste to form a circle in the centre of the pastry, approx. 5cm (2 inch) away from the sides. Arrange the plum slices on top.

3. Carefully fold over the pastry edge, pleating it as you go, to partially cover some of the filling. Press the pastry edge lightly to keep in place. Dot the plums with butter and sprinkle with Demerara sugar.

4. Brush the pastry with egg, and bake for about 40 mins until the pastry is golden and the plums tender. Best served warm.

Variation

You can use one of the flaky pastries for this type of Italian pie too. Roll out ½ quantity flaky or puff pastry to make a 30cm (12inch) round. Follow the method above, but only leave 2.5cm (1inch) clear pastry round the edge. Brush with egg and fold over the pastry over itself to make a rim. Press with a fork to seal, fill and brush with egg. Bake as above until the pastry is risen and crisp.

Gooseberry and Elderflower Jalousie

Serves: 4-6   Preparation: 30 mins plus cooling   Cooking: 30 mins

Pronounced "ja-loo-zee", this pastry dessert takes its name from the slatted effect on its lid, resembling a louvre or "jalousie" window.

1. Put the gooseberries in a saucepan with 75g (2½oz) sugar and 2 Tbsp water, bring to the boil, cover and simmer for 8–10 mins until softened but still holding shape. Leave to cool.

2. Whisk the egg yolk and 25g (1oz) sugar together until pale, thick and creamy. Whisk in the flour, cornflour and 2 Tbsp milk to make a smooth paste. Heat the remaining milk to just below boiling point and then pour over the egg and flour paste, whisking until smooth and well combined.

3. Transfer to a saucepan and stir over a low heat until boiling and then cook for a further 2 mins until thick. Cool for 10 mins, then mix in the cordial. Cover the surface with buttered greaseproof paper and leave to cool.

4. Preheat the oven to 220°C, 200°C fan oven, 425°F, gas 7. Line a large baking tray with baking parchment. Divide the pastry into two pieces. On a lightly floured surface roll one half to a 28 x 15cm (11 x 6inch) rectangle. Carefully transfer to the baking tray.

5. Spread with cold custard, leaving a 2.5cm (1inch) gap on both sides, and spoon over the gooseberries. Brush both edges with the egg white. Roll the other half of the pastry into a rectangle to slightly bigger than the bottom. Using a sharp knife, cut approx. 2cm (¾inch) wide slashes in the pastry across its width, leaving a 2cm (¾inch) border around the edge.

6. Lay the slatted pastry on the fruit and custard so that it opens slightly. Press down gently to seal. Knock up the edges and brush with egg white. Sprinkle with remaining sugar and bake for about 20 mins until golden. Serve warm or cold.

Ingredients

- 300g (10oz) firm green gooseberries, topped and tailed
- 115g (4oz) caster (superfine) sugar
- 1 egg, separated
- 1 Tbsp plain (all purpose) flour
- 1 Tbsp cornflour (cornstarch)
- 200ml (7fl.oz) whole milk
- 2 Tbsp elderflower cordial
- ½ quantity puff pastry

Moroccan Snake Pie (M'hanncha)

Serves: 6   Preparation: 40 mins plus cooling   Cooking: 40 mins

Ingredients

75g (2 ½ oz) shelled unsalted
    pistachios, very finely chopped
75g (2 ½ oz) blanched almonds,
    very finely chopped
75g (2 ½ oz) pitted dates,
    minced
75g (2 ½ oz) unsalted butter,
    melted
1 tsp good quality almond extract
100g (3 ½ oz) + 2 tsp icing
    (confectioner's) sugar
½ tsp finely grated orange rind
Approx. 4 tsp essence of pure
    orange blossom, optional
6 square sheets brick pastry or 6
    large sheets filo pastry
1 egg, beaten
1 tsp ground cinnamon

It was a toss-up between this recipe and Baklava as to which Middle Eastern-style pastry to include. In the end, I decided to give this one some exposure instead. Traditionally made with all nuts, I add dates for moistness. The name will certainly get everyone talking!

1. Put the nuts in a bowl and mix in the dates, all but 1 Tbsp melted butter, almond extract, 100g (3½oz) icing sugar and orange rind. Gradually add sufficient orange blossom essence to taste if using. Mix well to make a firm paste. Set aside.

2. Preheat the oven to 180°C, 160°C fan oven, 350°F, gas 4. Grease and line a 18cm (7inch) loose bottomed cake tin, and brush with remaining butter.

3. To use brick pastry, lay one sheet on the work surface shiny side down in front of you. Divide the almond filling into 6 equal pieces, and spread one portion of filling towards the bottom edge of the pastry, in a sausage shape along its length.

4. Roll up tightly in the pastry, brushing with water to seal and place inside the tin pushed snugly to the edge. Repeat with the remaining sheets and filling, laying the coils in the tin, side by side, so that they fill the tin as a complete coil.

5. If using filo pastry, lay out one sheet of pastry at a time on the work surface. Fold to make a square, then fill and roll as above.

6. Stand the tin on a baking tray, brush with egg and sprinkle with half the cinnamon. Bake for about 40 mins until crisp and golden.

7. Cool for 10 mins then carefully remove from the tin and transfer to a heatproof serving plate, dust the top with remaining icing sugar and cinnamon. Best served warm.

Loving Spoonful Puffs

Serves: 4 Preparation: 35 mins plus cooling Cooking: 55 mins

A variation on the vol au vent which can be filled with sweet and savoury fillings. A petal or flower shaped or star cutter works well too with this idea. Perfect for Valentine's Day or any meal for someone special.

1. Rinse the rice in a sieve under cold running water. Place in a saucepan, pour over the milk and slowly bring to the boil. Cover with the lid propped open on a wooden spoon handle and simmer very gently for about 35 mins, stirring occasionally, until soft and thick.

2. Remove from the heat, stir in the sugar and vanilla, and leave to cool. Discard the vanilla pod and add rosewater to taste.

3. Preheat the oven to 230°C, 210°C fan oven, 450°F, gas 8. Lightly grease a baking tray. Divide the pastry into 4 equal pieces and roll out each piece on a lightly floured surface to just large enough to allow you to cut out a 10cm (4inch) wide heart shape.

4. Cut part the way through the centre of each using a 7cm (2 ¾inch) wide heart cutter – this will form the lid. Transfer to the baking sheet. Brush the tops with beaten egg and bake for about 20 mins until risen and golden brown.

5. Carefully remove the inner hearts of pastry, keep and set aside. Scoop out the soft pastry from inside to leave crisp pastry shells. Cool the cases on a wire rack.

6. To serve, spoon the rice pudding into the cases to fill them. Sprinkle with pomegranate seeds; dust the lids with icing sugar and arrange the lids on top. Decorate with rose petals and serve immediately.

Ingredients

- 75g (2 ½ oz) short grain or pudding rice
- 450ml (¾ pt) whole milk
- 50g (2oz) caster (superfine) sugar
- 1 vanilla pod, split
- Approx. 1 ½ tsp essence of pure rosewater.
- 1 quantity puff pastry
- 1 egg, beaten, to glaze
- 2 Tbsp pomegranate seeds
- 1 tsp icing (confectioner's) sugar
- A few rose petals to decorate

Acknowledgements

I'd like to thank Amanda Brown for helping me with the recipe testing (and for making all that pastry for the photography sessions!) and to other friends and family who have helped me out with tasting my pie creations. I'm very grateful to Rachel Bass for providing me with a selection of her lovely pie birds for some of the photos, and to Ian Garlick for creating so many lovely images with my pies.

Bibliography

Colquhoun, Kate, *Taste*, Bloomsbury, 2007

Davidson, Alan, *The Oxford Companion of Food*, Oxford University Press, 1999

Good Housekeeping Cookery Book, compiled by The Good Housekeeping Institute,
        Ebury Press, 1983

Larousse Gastronomique, Paul Hamlyn, 1989

Mason, Laura with Catherine Brown, *Traditional Foods of Britain*, An Inventory,
        Prospect Books, 1999

McGee, Harold, *McGee on Food and Cooking*, Hodder and Stoughton, 2004

Ross, Robert and Scottish Meat Traders Association, *Scottish Meat Training:
        A Taste for Pastry – SMTA*, Perth, Scotland.